THE MAKING OF THE MOVIE

THE MAKING OF THE MOVIE

ANDREW DARLING

Reynolds & Hearn Ltd
London

ACKNOWLEDGEMENTS

Many thanks to Marcus Hearn and Richard Reynolds for giving me
the opportunity to write this book, and for much banter. Also, to
James King, whose work on its design has really brought it to life,
and to Kate Wyhowska for helping put the wheels in motion.

For their generosity in terms of time and help I'd like to say a big
'thank you' to Marit Allen, John Beard, Tim Bevan, Ray Chan,
Dominic Colenso, Ron Cook, Brady Corbet, Jonathan Frakes,
Marc Homes, Vanessa Hudgens, Rose Keegan, Dominic Lavery,
Peter Mountain, Sophia Myles, Deobia Oparei, Tanya Phegan,
Lex Shrapnel, Ben Torgersen, Mike Trim and Philip Winchester.

Thanks to Framestore CFC for their time and indulgence.
In particular, I would like to thank Fiona Chilton, Amy Crowther,
Piers Hampton and Lucy Killick, together with Jonathan Fawkner,
Craig Lyn, Justin Martin, Mike McGee and Mark Nelmes.

Thanks also to Matthew Redhead and Emma Cuthbert, for putting
me up countless times and for eating what I put in front of them,
and to Andrew Godfrey for invaluable pre-press support.
Also to Ruth, for everything else…

Finally, I'd like to say a big thank you to Alan Bromley, who introduced
me to Thunderbirds in the first place, some 20 years ago.

First published in 2004 by
Reynolds & Hearn Ltd
61a Priory Road
Kew Gardens
Richmond
Surrey TW9 3DH

A CIP catalogue record for this book is available from the British Library.

ISBN 1 903111 73 0

Designed by James King.

Printed and bound in Great Britain by Thanet Press Ltd, Margate, Kent.

CHAPTER FOUR

THE STORY

Billionaire ex-astronaut Jeff Tracy was grief-stricken when his wife was killed in a tragic accident. Jeff determined to use his wealth for the good of humanity and to establish a top secret organisation – International Rescue – dedicated to saving lives faced with disaster.

Recruiting eccentric genius Hyram 'Brains' Hackenbacker to support him in this effort, Jeff moved his family of five sons to the remote Pacific island that was to serve as the organisation's base. Once established there, work began on building five incredible craft – the Thunderbirds – that were to be the centrepieces of the operation.

Ten years on, while his elder brothers work alongside their father in the day-to-day running of International Rescue, the youngest Tracy – Alan – attends a private school. There he daydreams about one day becoming a Thunderbird pilot himself.

Alan is not on his own at the school. Brains' son Fermat is also a student, and it is he that races to tell Alan about a rescue operation being relayed, live, in the common room. The pair arrive there to see Thunderbirds 1 and 2 rescuing workers from an oil rig in the Bearing Straits.

The rescue only increases Alan's resentment of his situation, but he is lifted from his despair by the arrival of Lady Penelope – International Rescue's London agent. Accompanied by her trusty chauffeur Parker, she has been asked to take Alan back to Tracy Island for the holidays.

It is not long before the novelty of being home starts wearing off. Teased by his brothers, Alan walks off and, with Fermat's help, manages to disarm the security systems and break into Thunderbird 1's cockpit. Even Fermat's presence doesn't keep him out of trouble – he accidentally fires Thunderbird 1's engines and is called to his father's office for a dressing down.

Alan receives a scolding from Jeff Tracy, and Fermat tells his own father about a strange oily substance he discovered on Thunderbird 2's hull. Brains is intrigued and decides to investigate.

Unbeknownst to him, the substance is in fact a sophisticated tracer beacon. The oil rig disaster had been the result of an act of sabotage, undertaken by a mercenary named Mullion. The disaster had been created to draw International Rescue into a trap. Posing as one of the oil rig workers, Mullion had allowed himself to be rescued and had taken the opportunity to apply the substance to the vessel. Mullion is employed by a criminal mastermind known as The Hood. The brother of Jeff Tracy's housekeeper, Kyrano, The Hood is determined to destroy International Rescue. The tracer substance is used to identify the location of International Rescue's headquarters.

As Alan stalks away from his angry confrontation with his father, The Hood arrives at Tracy Island in a submarine. By listening to International Rescue's communications, The Hood's other employee – a brilliant woman named Transom – identifies the location of the organisation's orbiting space station, Thunderbird 5. In order to get the Tracys to evacuate the island, a missile is fired at the station.

The tactic works – Thunderbird 5 is badly damaged. Jeff and his four eldest sons race into action, climbing aboard Thunderbird 3 and launching into space. Alan only discovers what has happened when Fermat finds him on the beach where he is talking to Kyrano's daughter Tin-Tin. Tin-Tin's relationship with Alan has always been difficult, but the news of what has happened begins to draw the pair closer together.

Just as they are about to return to the house, the three children see The Hood's submarine rising out of the sea. By the time they get back to the compound, The Hood has taken control and disabled Thunderbird 5's life support systems. Trapped on the damaged space station, all of Alan's family are facing certain death.

Hiding in a ventilation shaft, the children learn what has happened and discover The Hood's plans to devastate the global financial system by breaking into the world's main banks. They manage to slow The Hood down by disabling Thunderbird 2, and are later helped by Lady Penelope and Parker. The Hood has mysterious mental powers, however, and the inhabitants of Tracy Island are unable to defeat him. The Hood captures the three children, locks them in the refrigerator with his other prisoners, and sets off with his minions to break into the Bank of London.

Fortunately, The Hood has not accounted for Parker's ingenuity. A one-time jailbird, the stout chauffeur uses his skills to break out of the fridge. With remarkable speed, control is returned to Thunderbird 5 and the lives of Alan's remaining family are saved. As they begin to take stock, Alan and company agree to follow The Hood to London in Thunderbird 1.

It is just as well that they do. Upon their arrival everything is in chaos. The Hood is using the the International Rescue vehicle the Mole to drill into the Bank of London's vaults. In the process, he has cut through a pylon supporting the London Monorail and a carriage, full of people, has plummeted into the Thames below.

Flying Thunderbird 2 into position, Alan leaves Fermat in charge and dives into the river in Thunderbird 4 – International Rescue's underwater vessel. With Tin-Tin's help, Alan manages to lift the carriage to safety.

By this point, Alan's father and brothers have arrived in the capital. The scene is set for a climactic confrontation between International Rescue and The Hood…

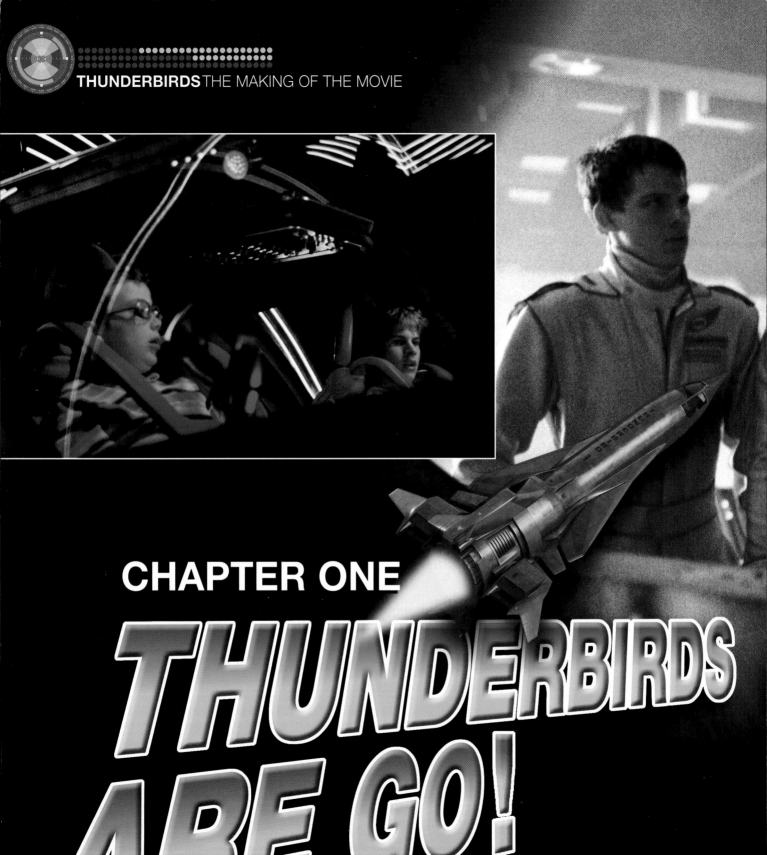

CHAPTER ONE

THUNDERBIRDS ARE GO!

FILMING on the
Thunderbirds movie began on 3 March 2003,
somewhere in the Seychelles. Production of the movie marked
the end of a long wait by dedicated *Thunderbirds* fans, who had
been anticipating the return of International Rescue for many years.

After two scouting trips and months of preparation and
organisation, six actors and a small army of filmmakers had travelled
half-way across the world. There, in an idyllic location in the Indian
Ocean, they were preparing to realise a long held dream.

Collectively, cast and crew were driven by a determination to bring
life back to a television series that had prematurely ended some 38
years earlier. No detail would be ignored, no decision would be made
lightly, no journey would be too short, in order for justice to be done
to this remarkable 1960s show.

Originally broadcast in 1965, *Thunderbirds* was a British-made
television series that starred an enchanting cast of beautifully crafted
puppets. Created by producer Gerry Anderson, and using a technique
called Supermarionation to bring the puppets to life, this endearing
television series ran for 32 episodes and two feature films.

Production of the puppet-based *Thunderbirds* adventures came to
an end in 1967, but the series has achieved a remarkable longevity.

Through
increasingly frequent
repeats and endless sales of *Thunderbirds*
toys, videos and DVDs, the series has been
embraced by successive generations of children.

Featuring the Tracy family – five brothers and their father, Jeff –
Thunderbirds followed the endeavours of their top secret organisation,
International Rescue, and its efforts to save the lives of people in
desperate need. With their super-sophisticated rescue vehicles,
this remarkable American family was able to reach crisis situations
anywhere in the globe within hours and avert countless tragedies.

The series' premise was audacious and altruistic, and although it
never received a network transmission in the United States, it made a
huge impact in the UK, Japan, and many other countries. Sadly, this
success wasn't sufficient for the series to continue in the longer term.
Although two feature films were made these were not commercially
successful, and part way through its second season, the series
came to an abrupt end.

VEHICLE PROFILE

THUNDERBIRD 1

The spearhead of all International Rescue disaster operations, Thunderbird 1 serves as the reconnaissance vessel for the fleet. Faster than the other craft – excepting Thunderbird 3 – Thunderbird 1 is always the first vehicle to arrive on the scene.

It is the responsibility of pilot Scott Tracy to use Thunderbird 1 to evaluate the disaster situation. Thunderbird 1's incredible manoeuvrability and relatively small size enables Scott to monitor a situation from above, dart forward quickly, or even approach a small space and peer inside. It also allows him to show off and perform triumphant victory rolls over the top of Thunderbird 2!

Thunderbird 1 is equipped with an array of monitoring equipment to help with Scott's disaster analysis. Heat sensors, infrared cameras, and sonar trackers, enable Scott to examine buildings or structures and even to analyse situations developing underwater.

Once he has gathered this information, Scott is ready to recommend a course of action to his father back at Tracy Island. These recommendations usually take the form of advice on what rescue equipment Thunderbird 2 should bring to bear and where this should be located. Scott may also offer directions to local rescue teams or individuals who are in peril. Scott will often remain in the disaster zone to oversee and lead the operation. During the oil rig disaster, Scott was required to target and fire a missile at the burning oil well in order to put it out. This operation required precision shooting, but despite the appalling conditions he managed it with ease. This is typical of Scott's self-assured manner, but he was of course helped by Thunderbird 1's state-of-the-art targeting computers!

COCKPIT

To maximise pilot visibility, Thunderbird 1 has a 360° transparent cockpit. This allows the pilot to directly monitor events taking place both above and below the craft. In order to make the ship as accessible as possible, the lower cockpit windows fold outwards and the pilot and co-pilot seats are lowered through them and down onto the ground. In emergencies, the ability to get on and off a ship quickly is essential. This is why Brains integrated this feature into the final design.

STBD. ENGINE THRUST

74

74

PERCENT

MAX

FLAPS

FLAPS ADJUST
·DEGREES·

NOSE CONE

Thunderbird 1 can
reach amazing speeds
of Mach 20 or more.
During high velocity journeys the
vehicle's hull becomes incredibly hot.
Unsurprisingly, it is the craft's nose cone
that bears the brunt of these high temperatures.
Fortunately, the nose cone is constructed of an
alloy specially developed by Brains to withstand
these conditions without cracking or buckling.

SPECIFICATIONS

LENGTH: 80 feet
WINGSPAN: 30 feet
WEIGHT: 140 tons
MAXIMUM SPEED: 15,000 mph
CRUISING ALTITUDE: 150,000 feet
RECOMMENDED CREW: 1
PASSENGERS: 3

Over subsequent decades, repeated efforts were made to bring life back to the marionettes. The closest anyone got to reviving *Thunderbirds* was Tim Bevan at Working Title, the production company responsible for *Four Weddings and a Funeral* (1994) and *Notting Hill* (1999) among many others. In 1997, Working Title purchased the film rights to *Thunderbirds* from then-rights holders PolyGram. Notwithstanding a significant investment – a script and a team of concept artists working on designs for some five months – initial pre-production efforts came to nothing.

The film had been slated to be directed by Peter Hewitt – lately of *Thunderpants* (2002) and *The Borrowers* (1997) – and was to feature Pete Postlethwaite as Parker and Kristin Scott Thomas as Lady Penelope. Postlethwaite had come to international prominence in *The Lost World: Jurassic Park* (1997) while audiences were familiar with Thomas from her role in *Four Weddings and a Funeral*.

'We assumed too much prior knowledge about *Thunderbirds*,' says Bevan, reflecting on the original attempt. 'What we realised after we had developed it is that we hadn't really considered our core audience for the film. At the end of the day, most of the world don't actually know what *Thunderbirds* is.'

In late 2000, Working Title renewed their efforts, confident they had now found the right approach. Reviewing the original television series, Bevan and his colleagues agreed that the show was designed for children, not adults. They also determined that they needed a story that could introduce *Thunderbirds* to the nine tenths of the world that had never seen it. It was decided to base the film on a story set some years before the events of the television series. The audience would be introduced to International Rescue, the Thunderbird craft, and Tracy Island through the youngest Tracy brother's rite-of-passage.

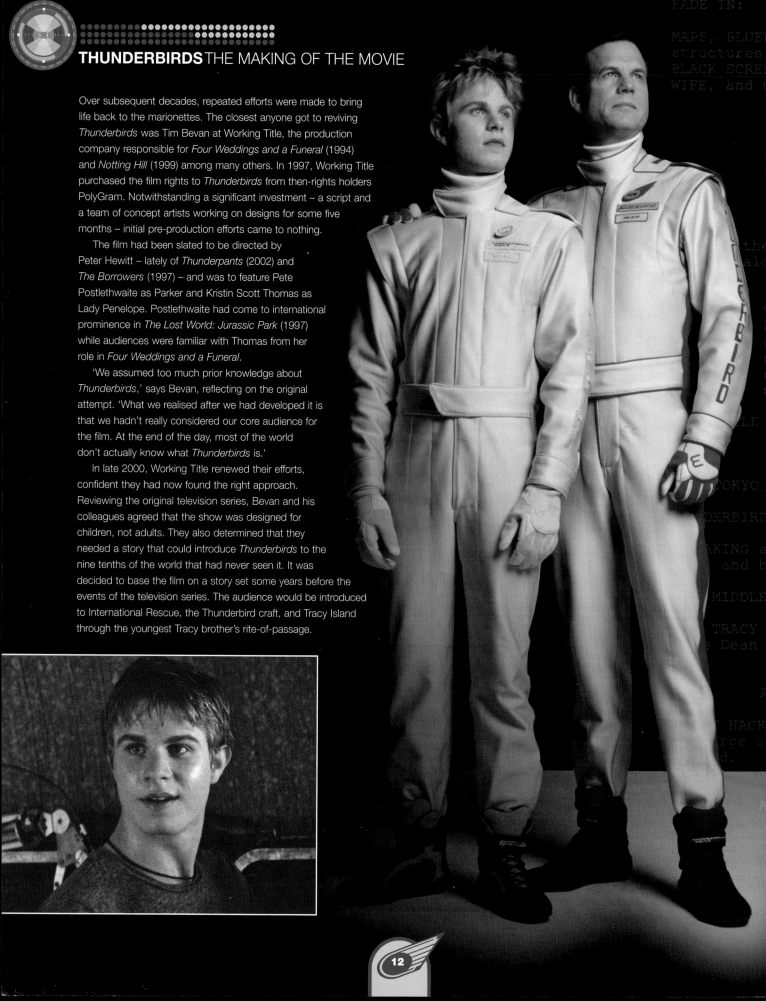

WRITING THE SCRIPT

Bevan began plotting out the story for the new *Thunderbirds* movie with Debra Heywood, the Head of Development at Working Title. After a series of meetings and discussions, the story was passed over to screenwriter William Osborne, who prepared a first draft script.

Everything rested on the script being right. Before Working Title could even begin expending further funds on the project, they needed a screenplay they could be sure would appeal to an audience. Although Bevan and his colleagues approved of the structure of Osborne's script, it was felt that the tone of the piece was a little flat. The magic of the original television series was missing.

Fortunately, in the modern movie-making world it is rare for a script to be right first time. Developing screenplays is an increasingly collaborative process, and it is common practice to bring in other writers to tweak the first draft, to bring the script up a notch.

Over the years Michael McCullers has gained a reputation as a script finisher. With previous experience on the *Austin Powers* movies and *Undercover Brother* (2002) he is adept at taking an initial script and playing with the dialogue, the interaction between the characters, and helping them to live on the page. It was this skill that Tim Bevan asked McCullers to bring to bear on the script.

PROFILE TIM BEVAN – PRODUCER

Tim Bevan has been involved in every stage of *Thunderbirds'* production, from the development of the story to overseeing the script's evolution, and from casting and filming, right through to the development of the visual effects.

Co-chaired by Tim Bevan and Eric Fellner since its establishment in 1982, Working Title Films is Europe's leading film production company. The company has produced more than 70 films, with a combined worldwide gross in excess of two and a half billion dollars, won four Academy Awards™, 20 British Academy Awards and numerous prizes at the Cannes and Berlin Film Festivals. In 2004, the company was awarded the prestigious Michal Balcon Bafta Award for its outstanding contribution to the British film industry.

Working Title is currently in post-production on *Bridget Jones: The Edge of Reason*, directed by Beeban Kidron with Renee Zellweger, Colin Firth and Hugh Grant; and *Wimbledon*, a romantic comedy starring Kirsten Dunst and Paul Bettany and directed by Richard Loncraine.

INTRODUCING THE THUNDERBIRDS

It is the opening sequence of *Thunderbirds* that has changed most radically since William Osborne's first draft.

Originally, the movie was to open with a dream sequence in which Alan would be flying Thunderbird 1, at speed, through a series of canyons. He would arrive at a Mount Rushmore in which one of the faces resembled his best friend, Fermat. Out of control, Thunderbird 1 would crash into Fermat's effigy and the rock face would begin crumbling. At this point, Alan would wake up.

Although this opening was retained for quite some time, it was eventually felt that its impact would be limited because the audience had not been introduced to the Thunderbirds, or to Fermat.

Instead, the idea of a bike chase, involving Alan and some of his school rivals, was introduced. Although much of this sequence was filmed, it was later felt that it delayed the introduction of International Rescue too much.

It was finally decided to bring the oil rig disaster right to the front of the movie. Intercut with scenes of Alan and Fermat watching the rescue on television, this sequence introduced Alan and the Thunderbirds at the same time.

As pre-production continued, Working Title sought a studio willing to provide backing and distribution. It was time to take the idea to their partner, Universal Studios.

The return of the Tracy brothers, International Rescue and the Thunderbirds, was back on the cards. It had taken months of work but finally, after four decades of waiting, *Thunderbirds* were go.

CONCLUDING SCENES

Like the opening scenes, the last 15 minutes of the first draft screenplay were also subject to significant change.

Originally, The Hood was going to land the stolen Thunderbird 2 in Parliament Square, right next to the Houses of Parliament. Eventually though, mounting security concerns meant that the production team were forbidden from filming there and they were obliged to think again.

It was then that the idea of Thunderbird 2 landing in London's Jubilee Gardens came to the fore. The Hood could land there and, in the process of piloting the Mole to the bank vault, cause the London Eye to tip forward, one of its lowermost pods dipping under the Thames and threatening the lives of its occupants. Unfortunately the Eye's owners, British Airways, refused to give permission for it to be depicted in this way.

The production team accordingly developed alternative ideas. In one of these the Mole would cause a London Underground tube line to become flooded. That idea was discarded when it was felt that there would be more excitement if the disaster took place in the open air.

It was then that the idea of a monorail, running across the Thames, began to be mooted. This time, as The Hood drilled his way to the Bank of London, one of the monorail pylons would be struck and a carriage would fall into the river.

The idea of a monorail was extremely appealing because it shifted the action away from the claustrophobic confines of the Underground and placed it firmly in the realm of a future London. An additional bonus was that no permission was required to knock over this part of the capital's infrastructure!

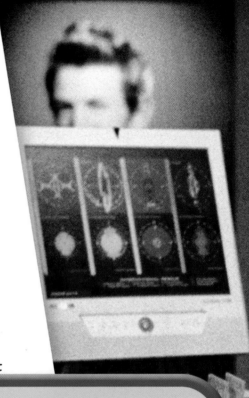

THUNDERBIRDS

by
William Osborne

Revisions by Michael McCullers

FADE IN:

MAPS, BLUEPRINTS and SCHEMATICS of futuristic structures built into an exotic island flash across a BLACK SCREEN, along with images of JEFF TRACY, HIS WIFE, and CHILDREN.

> VOICE OVER
> In the year two thousand and ten billionaire ex-astronaut Jeff Tracy lost his wife in a tragic accident. Consumed by grief, he took his five sons to an uncharted tropical island to rebuild their lives.

And now the BLUEPRINTS show amazing [?] we move along the side of a fantastic

> VOICE OVER
> There, in her memory, he bui[?] headquarters of Internationa[?] organization dedicated to h[?] need wherever and whenever [?] strikes. They have come to [?] name they gave their incre[?]

THUNDERBIRDS!

MAIN TITLE

EXT. TOKYO CITY SKYLINE - NIGHT

THUNDERBIRDS 1 AND 2 - IN A TIGHT

STREAKING across the city. They s[?] ROLL, and blast off in different

EXT. MIDDLE OF THE WOODS - UPSTA[?]

ALAN TRACY - he's 14, tousled hai[?] James Dean with a retainer.

> VOICE (O.S)
> A...A...Alan? Alan!

PROFILE WILLIAM OSBORNE – WRITER

William Osborne's debut as a screenwriter came with the smash hit comedy *Twins* (1988), starring Arnold Schwarzenegger and Danny DeVito as unlikely birth-mates. Since then, Osborne has also had success with the Sylvester Stallone vehicle *Stop! Or My Mom Will Shoot* (1992), *Dr Jekyll and Ms Hyde* (1995) and, most recently, *The Scorpion King* (2002). Written alongside Jonathan Hales – who co-wrote the *Star Wars* film *Attack of the Clones* with George Lucas – *The Scorpion King* is the spin-off prequel to *The Mummy Returns* (2001).

Following detailed story conferences with Tim Bevan and Debra Heywood, it was Osborne's job to turn their story into the first draft of the *Thunderbirds* screenplay.

PROFILEMICHAEL McCULLERS
– WRITER

Over the years, this well respected writer has gained a
reputation for his ability to hone and polish scripts. Best
known for the *Austin Powers* movies, McCullers worked
with Mike Myers on the screenplay for all three films,
from *International Man of Mystery* (1997) to
Goldmember (2002).

McCullers has also received screen credits for
Undercover Brother (2002), the spoof blaxploitation movie,
and *Curious George* which is due to be released in 2005.
On *Thunderbirds*, McCullers' role was to take Osborne's
script and to sharpen the dialogue, to help bring the
characters to life.

CHAPTER TWO

TEAM BUILDING

ONCE the script had been developed to Working Title's satisfaction, it was time to find a director. Tim Bevan was looking for a number of things when making this choice.

Bevan realised that cracking the American market would be crucial to the film's success. For this reason he was looking for someone with an intimate understanding of that audience.

The nature of *Thunderbirds* meant that there was going to be a considerable amount of visual effects. Working Title had never produced a movie that was so effects-intensive, and they needed a director with some experience in this field.

Additionally, there was a recognition that for the film to work it needed a number of big name actors, but they would only come on board if the director was someone with whom they would feel comfortable.

Tim Bevan's final criteria went right to the heart of Working Title's philosophy. Bevan calls this 'Making the bull's eye bigger': 'Too often with British films you load the odds against yourself, or as we say you make the bull's eye very, very small. You pick a somewhat quirky subject for a film and you get great actors but they may not be well known, and all the time the bull's eye for the success of that film is getting smaller and smaller and smaller.'

Bevan approached Jonathan Frakes to direct the film. An American with a considerable amount of effects experience from his work on the *Star Trek* television series and films, Frakes also had a reputation as an actors' director – someone whom actors enjoyed and wanted to work with. What's more, Frakes had a substantial following in *Star Trek* fandom, which could only help to raise the profile of the movie.

Hitting the bull's eye was beginning to look increasingly possible.

TE CONTROL DATA

PAYLOAD DATA

DIAGNOSTICS

THUNDERBIRD 2

INTERNATIONAL RESCUE

THUNDERBIRD 2

A behemoth of the skies, this huge craft is capable of transporting heavy duty rescue equipment in all weathers, to anywhere on the planet. Although slower than Thunderbird 1, its 5,000 mph is still some seven times the speed of sound – incredible given the kind of burdens that it carries.

What is even more remarkable is Thunderbird 2's manoeuvrability. Onlookers watching it sweep into London's Jubilee Gardens would have found it hard to credit the size and weight of this craft.

Of course, speed and manoeuvrability don't come without a price, and Thunderbird 2 is not an easy vehicle to fly. To minimise piloting errors, all pilot instructions are fed through four flight computers which vote on whether to accept them or not. If more than one computer votes against the instructions, they are ignored. As a result of this system, Thunderbird 2 is deemed exceptionally safe.

Thunderbird 2's launch platform on Tracy Island allows it to accelerate to maximum speed and acceleration within minutes of taking off. However, it does not have to rely on that launch facility to get off the ground. A series of vertical thrusters, combined with an anti-gravity engine, allow

AIRFOIL

With its huge mass and colossal size, Thunderbird 2 is an extremely difficult craft to fly, even with its on board computer systems. When hovering above a disaster or coming into land, the airfoil is vital in helping the pilot to steer it safely and accurately.

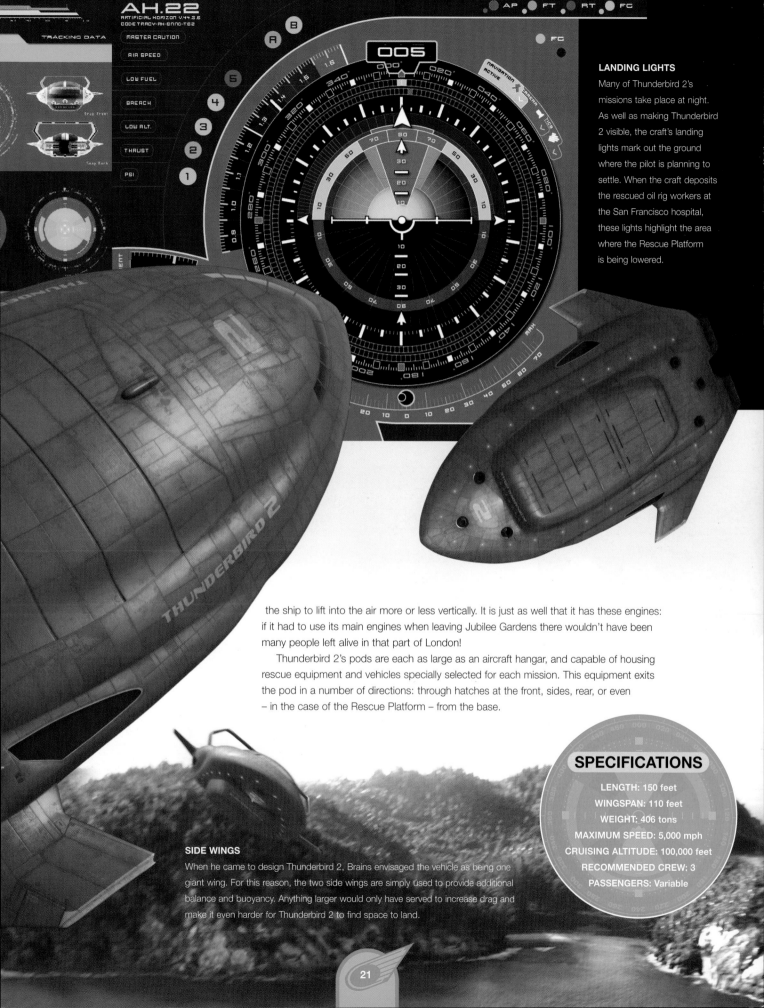

AH.22
ARTIFICIAL HORIZON V.44.3.6
CODE TRACY-AH-ENNO-T62

AP · FT · RT · FG

FG

MASTER CAUTION

AIR SPEED

LOW FUEL

BREACH

LOW ALT.

THRUST

PSI

TRACKING DATA

Drop Front

Snap Back

005

NAVIGATION ACTIVE

LANDING LIGHTS

Many of Thunderbird 2's missions take place at night. As well as making Thunderbird 2 visible, the craft's landing lights mark out the ground where the pilot is planning to settle. When the craft deposits the rescued oil rig workers at the San Francisco hospital, these lights highlight the area where the Rescue Platform is being lowered.

the ship to lift into the air more or less vertically. It is just as well that it has these engines: if it had to use its main engines when leaving Jubilee Gardens there wouldn't have been many people left alive in that part of London!

Thunderbird 2's pods are each as large as an aircraft hangar, and capable of housing rescue equipment and vehicles specially selected for each mission. This equipment exits the pod in a number of directions: through hatches at the front, sides, rear, or even – in the case of the Rescue Platform – from the base.

SIDE WINGS

When he came to design Thunderbird 2, Brains envisaged the vehicle as being one giant wing. For this reason, the two side wings are simply used to provide additional balance and buoyancy. Anything larger would only have served to increase drag and make it even harder for Thunderbird 2 to find space to land.

SPECIFICATIONS

LENGTH: 150 feet
WINGSPAN: 110 feet
WEIGHT: 406 tons
MAXIMUM SPEED: 5,000 mph
CRUISING ALTITUDE: 100,000 feet
RECOMMENDED CREW: 3
PASSENGERS: Variable

21

THUNDERBIRDS THE MAKING OF THE MOVIE

CASTING THE CREW

For Jonathan Frakes, the decision to work on this British movie was to bring with it a unique challenge. In order to secure key tax breaks, the film could only employ a very small number of non-UK or Commonwealth cast and crew. For this reason, Frakes was unable to bring with him any of the people with whom he had worked on previous projects. Frakes' effects supervisor, his director of photography, his

production designer, even his personal assistant, were not able to join him. Frakes was at least able to bring his wife, Genie Francis, and their two children from Los Angeles.

Frakes knew that casting his crew was just as important as casting actors: 'If the crew doesn't get along, or if they're butting heads about production versus lighting or costume versus sets, it's so counterproductive,' he says. Frakes selected his colleagues very carefully, aware that he would be working alongside some of them for almost two years.

CASTING HIMSELF

Having been raised as an actor, Jonathan Frakes has never been able to resist stepping in front of the camera. Although he has admitted that it is extremely difficult – 'you have to be surrounded by people you trust' – there aren't many things that he has directed and not appeared in.

The television series *Roswell*, on which he served as executive producer, is a case in point. In the show's pilot Frakes featured as the master of ceremonies at a festival, while in the episodes 'Convention' and 'Secrets and Lies' he appears as himself.

If you watch closely, Frakes can also be glimpsed playing a bystander in *Clockstoppers* (2002), his first non-*Star Trek* foray into cinema. In the final scenes of *Thunderbirds*, outside the Bank of London, Frakes can be seen playing a policeman.

PROFILE JONATHAN FRAKES – DIRECTOR

Ebullient and self-deprecating, Jonathan Frakes is recognised by *Star Trek* fans the world over as Commander William Riker. Before landing the role as first officer of the USS Enterprise, Frakes was best known for his portrayal of the character Stanley Hazard in *North and South*, the mini-series about the American Civil War which spawned two sequels.

Although many doubted whether *Star Trek: The Next Generation* would ever be successful, Frakes' role on the show brought with it a wealth of opportunity. After spending hundreds of hours in the editing suite, watching the series' many directors at work, Frakes took the opportunity to direct an episode himself.

By the end of the series' run on the small screen Frakes had been responsible for no less than seven hours of *Star Trek*. Frakes' sure hand and relaxed, yet efficient, approach earned him the nick-name 'two takes Frakes', and his directorial style became popular with cast, crew and producers.

It was for this reason that he was offered the director's chair for the second and third *Next Generation* movies – *First Contact* (1996) and *Insurrection* (1998). The critical and commercial success of the former gave Frakes the credibility he needed to step away from the *Star Trek* franchise.

Following *Insurrection*, Frakes spent some time as executive producer of sci-fi drama *Roswell*, before directing the childrens' movie, *Clockstoppers* (2002).

Frakes' decision to take on *Thunderbirds* and decamp his entire family to London was in large part enabled by his wife, Genie Francis. A regular for some 25 years on the daytime soap opera *General Hospital*, Francis expressed her willingness to move away from Los Angeles.

Looking back over the last two years, Frakes is slightly uncertain how he managed to land his job on *Thunderbirds*. After being sent tapes of the original Supermarionation series by his manager, Frakes began watching episodes with his two children and began realising just how full of possibility they were. 'I absorbed the shows with my kids,' he says. 'My daughter, who was five, loved Lady Penelope and asked to re-see episodes with her, and my son, who was eight, really wanted to fly or drive Thunderbird 4, while I loved the sense of altruism and danger without violence.'

After that, things just started falling into place. With no regrets about the move to London, he currently sees himself staying there for a good time yet.

Recognising that the people he was talking to had only got where they were because they were good at their jobs, Frakes concentrated on looking for individuals with whom he could share a rapport; individuals with whom he felt he could develop a strong, positive relationship.

Unfortunately, the risk surrounding the film wasn't about to end with Frakes' relative inexperience in the British film industry. As a result of conversations with producer Mark Huffam he suggested a number of other gambles.

Huffam had devised a number of innovative ideas, intended to make the filming process easier. Crucially though, as far as Frakes and Huffam knew, these ideas had not been attempted before. Huffam's first idea related to the pre-visualisation of the movie. Traditionally, set-piece films like *Thunderbirds* are

storyboarded, and then the storyboards are animated so that the director and producers can get a feel for the flow of the movie. This work is called pre-visualisation.

Usually, this 'pre-vis' work is undertaken by one company that specialises in this area, while a different company is brought in to produce the visual effects themselves.

Huffam's suggestion was that they employ the same company to do both the pre-vis and the visual effects – in other words, to stay with the production from beginning to end. The hope was that this level of involvement would lead to significant time-savings during post-production. On paper this made sense, but there was still a nagging doubt that the production team were just making things difficult for themselves.

PROFILE MARK HUFFAM – PRODUCER

Jonathan Frakes credits Mark Huffam with some of the most innovative thinking behind the production of *Thunderbirds*. The inspiration for these ideas was the result of many years of experience in the film industry.

Huffam has made a name for himself on a number of movies, ranging from *The Hours* (2002) – starring Meryl Streep, Nicole Kidman, and Julianne Moore – and Phillip Kauffman's *Quills* (2000), to the Rowan Atkinson vehicle *Johnny English*. This eclectic range is similar to that of many other people on the production.

In the early stages of the film's development, Huffam had particular responsibility for location scouting, travelling all over the world with location manager Pierre Harter, and later Jonathan Frakes and production designer John Beard.

Huffam's second idea grew from the first. In traditional productions, the effects house and design team work independently from each other, the effects house simply being handed the designs as a *fait accompli* and obliged to run with them. However, if the effects house was going to be involved throughout pre-production, why not get them and the designers working together as one team, developing the designs in a more collaborative manner?

The choice of effects house was going to be critical to the success of Huffam's ideas. Making this choice is always the single most expensive decision ever made in movies like *Thunderbirds*, but twinned with Huffam's other ideas, everything was riding on their choice being the right one.

The decision was even more important because, in *Thunderbirds*, the visuals were as important as the script. In many ways, the Thunderbird craft were the essence of the original television series – the ships were effectively characters in their own right. The expectations of several generations of adults were riding on these ships being well realised. Whoever eventually got the job had a lot to live up to. After much discussion, it became obvious that Framestore CFC would be the best choice.

PROFILEMARK NELMES AND MIKE McGEE – VISUAL EFFECTS SUPERVISORS

Mark Nelmes (pictured right) and Mike McGee (left) are both veterans of the visual effects industry, although it would be fair to say that neither has worked on anything of the size and scale of *Thunderbirds*.

Framestore CFC's contribution to the movie has been so significant that both McGee and Nelmes have been credited in the film's main title sequence. Appearing there is against the rules of the Director's Guild of America, and a special appeal was lodged in order to secure this.

Mike McGee was part of the team that established Framestore CFC in 1987. Since then he has seen the company grow from four to 450 people and merge with CFC. McGee's own success in the business was recognised when he won an Emmy for his work on the American mini-series *The Odyssey*. After completing that work, McGee worked on the fictional documentary series *Walking with Dinosaurs* and Hallmark's *Dinotopia*.

Alongside Mark Nelmes, McGee has been responsible or overseeing all the visual effects on *Thunderbirds*. Despite the range of his experience on a variety of TV series, *Thunderbirds* was his first feature film and marked a small step into the unknown.

Mark Nelmes has worked on everything from Kenneth Branagh's *Frankenstein* (1994) to *The End of the Affair* (1999) and *The Mummy Returns* (2001). Nelmes sees the approach to *Thunderbirds* as being quite different to other movies. Whereas visual effects artists are generally proudest of the effects people don't notice, this doesn't apply with *Thunderbirds*. As Nelmes says, 'This is a kids' film, so if you can't see the effects you've failed.'

As well as overseeing the digital effects, Mark was also responsible for shooting the model of the oil rig and the various explosions that take place over and around it.

Even so, there were some risks involved in this decision. In most movies, an independent visual effects supervisor would work for the director and interface with the effects house. Indeed, on his previous films, Frakes had always had his own visual effects supervisors – John Knoll in the case of *Star Trek: First Contact* and Jim Rygiel for *Star Trek: Insurrection*.

For *Thunderbirds*, Frakes agreed to go with Framestore CFC's Mark Nelmes and Mike McGee. The task ahead of them was formidable. Framestore CFC had agreed to produce all of the film's effects shots – more CGI shots than had ever previously been realised by any effects house in Europe. The production was depending on Framestore CFC undertaking all the pre-visualisation, working as one with the production design team, and producing every single optical in the movie. What's more, Frakes was relying on Framestore CFC's own supervisors to realise his vision.

A HIGH BAR

'I had worked with the very best in that field so I had a very high bar for that kind of work,' says Frakes, talking about the decision to choose Framestore CFC to produce the film's visual effects.

On *Star Trek: First Contact* Frakes' visual effects supervisor had been John Knoll. It was immediately after completing that movie that Knoll went on to supervise the effects on George Lucas' *Star Wars* prequel *The Phantom Menace*. He has gone on to supervise the two subsequent instalments in the prequel trilogy. In between those movies, Knoll also worked on *Deep Blue Sea* (1999) and *Pirates of the Caribbean: The Curse of the Black Pearl* (2003).

For Frakes' second movie – *Star Trek: Insurrection* – Jim Rygiel served as his visual effects supervisor. Rygiel would later work on Peter Jackson's *The Lord of the Rings* trilogy, the only project that could rival the *Star Wars* prequels for ambition or complexity in terms of visual effects.

With Frakes having worked with such visual effects luminaries, Framestore CFC had a huge amount to live up to – could they possibly meet that standard?

THE HOVERBIKE CHASE

With Thunderbird 5 crippled and Tracy Island overrun by The Hood, Alan, Fermat and Tin-Tin hike up to Satellite Hill. There they attempt to return control to International Rescue's space station. However, despite Fermat's best efforts, Transom discovers what they are doing and blocks their jerry-rigged signal.

As they race back down the island, chased by Mullion, the three children come across a damaged hoverbike and sled. Fermat is concerned about the hoverbike's condition and its connection to the sled is precarious – for these reasons he tells Alan not to travel too fast. Of course, Alan wants to be a hero, just like his brothers. What's more, Mullion is charging through the

jungle behind them and the lives of his family are at risk. He ignores Fermat's warnings and starts pushing the hoverbike to its limits.

As they fly through the jungle and down the hillside, the connection between bike and sled begins to weaken. Before long, the sled detaches, leaving Tin-Tin and Fermat behind.

Mullion's own progress does not slow – in moments he reaches them and seizes Tin-Tin and Fermat before they can recover from their fall. Alan manages to avoid Mullion for the time being but it won't be long before he too is captured…

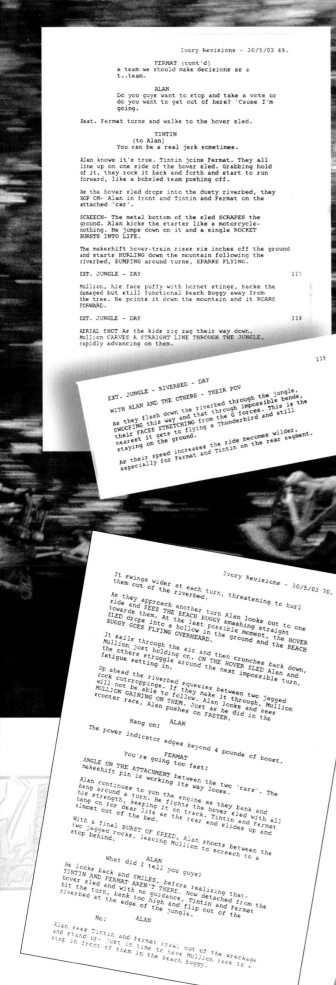

Ivory Revisions - 30/5/03 69.

FERMAT (cont'd)
a team we should make decisions as a
t..team.

ALAN
Do you guys want to stop and take a vote or
do you want to get out of here? 'Cause I'm
going.

Beat. Fermat turns and walks to the hover sled.

TINTIN
(to Alan)
You can be a real jerk sometimes.

Alan knows it's true. Tintin joins Fermat. They all
line up on one side of the hover sled. Grabbing hold
of it, they rock it back and forth and start to run
forward, like a bobsled team pushing off.

As the hover sled drops into the dusty riverbed, they
HOP ON- Alan in front and Tintin and Fermat on the
attached 'car'.

SCREECH- The metal bottom of the sled SCRAPES the
ground. Alan kicks the starter like a motorcycle-
nothing. He jumps down on it and a single ROCKET
BURSTS INTO LIFE.

The makeshift hover-train rises six inches off the ground
and starts HURLING down the mountain following the
riverbed, BUMPING around turns, SPARKS FLYING.

EXT. JUNGLE - DAY   117

Mullion, his face puffy with hornet stings, backs the
damaged but still functional Beach Buggy away from
the tree. He points it down the mountain and it ROARS
FORWARD.

EXT. JUNGLE - DAY   118

AERIAL SHOT As the kids zig zag their way down,
Mullion CARVES A STRAIGHT LINE THROUGH THE JUNGLE,
rapidly advancing on them.

119

EXT. JUNGLE - RIVERBED - DAY

WITH ALAN AND THE OTHERS - THEIR POV

As they flash down the riverbed through the jungle,
SWOOPING this way and that through impossible bends,
their FACES STRETCHING from the G forces. This is the
nearest it gets to flying a Thunderbird and still
staying on the ground.

As their speed increases the ride becomes wilder,
especially for Fermat and Tintin on the rear segment.

Ivory Revisions - 30/5/03 70.

It swings wider at each turn, threatening to hurl
them out of the riverbed.

As they approach another turn Alan looks out to one
side and SEES THE BEACH BUGGY smashing straight
towards them. At the last possible moment, the HOVER
SLED drops into a hollow in the ground and the BEACH
BUGGY GOES FLYING OVERHEAD.

It sails through the air and then crunches back down,
Mullion just holding on. ON THE HOVER SLED Alan and
the others struggle around the next impossible turn,
fatigue setting in.

Up ahead the riverbed squeezes between two jagged
rock outcroppings. If they make it through, Mullion
will not be able to follow. Alan looks and sees
MULLION GAINING ON THEM. Just as he did in the
scooter race, Alan pushes on FASTER.

ALAN
Hang on!

The power indicator edges beyond 4 pounds of boost.

FERMAT
You're going too fast!

ANGLE ON THE ATTACHMENT between the two 'cars'. The
makeshift pin is working its way loose.

Alan continues to gun the engine as they bank and
hang around a turn. He fights the hover sled with all
his strength, keeping it on track. Tintin and Fermat
hang on for dear life as the rear end slides up and
almost out of the bed.

With a final BURST OF SPEED, Alan shoots between the
two jagged rocks, leaving Mullion to screech to a
stop behind.

ALAN
What did I tell you guys?

He looks back and SMILES, before realizing that-
TINTIN AND FERMAT AREN'T THERE. Now detached from the
hover sled and with no guidance, Tintin and Fermat
hit the turn, bank too high and flip out of the
riverbed at the edge of the jungle.

ALAN
No!

Alan sees Tintin and Fermat crawl out of the wreckage
and stand up- just in time to have Mullion race to a
stop in front of them in the Beach Buggy.

DESIGN BRIEF

One of the reasons Working Title invited Jonathan Frakes to direct *Thunderbirds* was his experience of working on *Star Trek*. The following which that series has developed, and the high expectations of *Star Trek* fandom, had resulted in considerable pressure being brought to bear on producers, directors and stars alike. Over the years, Frakes had shown that he was more than comfortable at dealing with this.

Unsurprisingly, *Thunderbirds* fans are equally passionate about the original Gerry Anderson series and protective of Anderson's legacy. Frakes was certainly sensitive to this: '*Thunderbirds* is huge here!' he says. 'The reaction to the show in the UK is so contagious and upbeat and people are so excited about the movie that I just got caught up in the whole thing.'

Much of this expectation rested on the work of the design department. The look of the original series, with its outrageous and distinctive vehicles, was what everyone remembers most about it. For this reason, the visual side of the movie was as important as the script. Frakes had selected John Beard to be his production designer, and it was down to Beard and his team to recreate the magic of the original series.

Of course, Beard wasn't starting from scratch. During their 1997 effort to produce a *Thunderbirds* film, Working Title had commissioned three concept artists to capture the overall look and feel they were aiming for. However, as a result of discussions with Jonathan Frakes it became clear that this movie would be going in a very different direction.

Frakes was very attracted by the vibrant primary colours of the original series. 'I wanted the film to "pop" not just literally – pop culture – but also figuratively. I wanted people's eyes to pop open.' The designs developed in 1997, although good, were not really

intended to achieve this. The vehicles were very over-engineered, and Frakes and Beard were keen to take a more 'designed' route.

One of the ideas that became a catch-phrase for the movie was 'retro-modernism'. References that were used repeatedly included vehicles like the new Mini and the redesigned VW Beetle. These were both 1960s designs that had recently been dusted down and updated for a new generation. The designs for *Thunderbirds* would share a similar aim.

PROFILEJOHN BEARD – PRODUCTION DESIGNER

It is easy to assume that the production designer for *Thunderbirds* would be someone with an extensive track record in designing fantasy and science fiction films. 'Beard's an interesting cat: he brought a very interesting, eclectic build to the movie so it's not just all pop culture,' says Frakes. 'His personality is not all kids in spaceships; it's informed, with some history, and that has made his designs much richer.'

Eclectic is certainly a watch-word for Beard's career. He has worked on films as diverse as Monty Python's *The Life of Brian* (1979), *Wings of the Dove* (1997) and *Enigma* (2001).

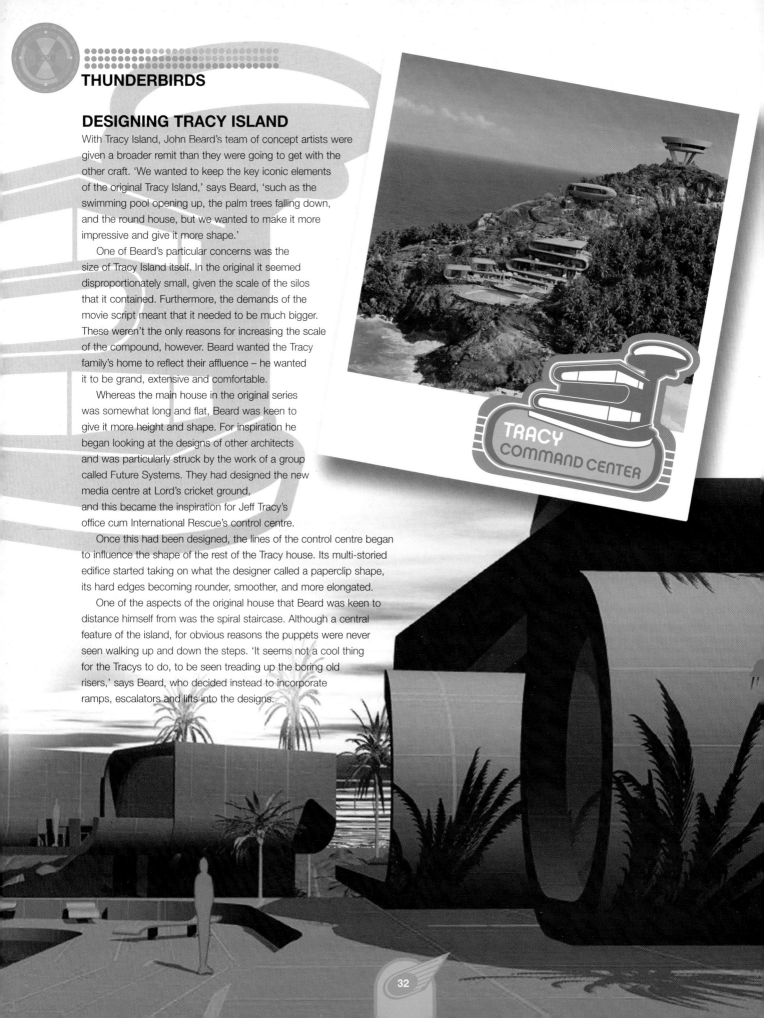

THUNDERBIRDS

DESIGNING TRACY ISLAND

With Tracy Island, John Beard's team of concept artists were given a broader remit than they were going to get with the other craft. 'We wanted to keep the key iconic elements of the original Tracy Island,' says Beard, 'such as the swimming pool opening up, the palm trees falling down, and the round house, but we wanted to make it more impressive and give it more shape.'

One of Beard's particular concerns was the size of Tracy Island itself. In the original it seemed disproportionately small, given the scale of the silos that it contained. Furthermore, the demands of the movie script meant that it needed to be much bigger. These weren't the only reasons for increasing the scale of the compound, however. Beard wanted the Tracy family's home to reflect their affluence – he wanted it to be grand, extensive and comfortable.

Whereas the main house in the original series was somewhat long and flat, Beard was keen to give it more height and shape. For inspiration he began looking at the designs of other architects and was particularly struck by the work of a group called Future Systems. They had designed the new media centre at Lord's cricket ground, and this became the inspiration for Jeff Tracy's office cum International Rescue's control centre.

Once this had been designed, the lines of the control centre began to influence the shape of the rest of the Tracy house. Its multi-storied edifice started taking on what the designer called a paperclip shape, its hard edges becoming rounder, smoother, and more elongated.

One of the aspects of the original house that Beard was keen to distance himself from was the spiral staircase. Although a central feature of the island, for obvious reasons the puppets were never seen walking up and down the steps. 'It seems not a cool thing for the Tracys to do, to be seen treading up the boring old risers,' says Beard, who decided instead to incorporate ramps, escalators and lifts into the designs.

TRACY COMMAND CENTER

Given how familiar rocket and shuttle launches have become in recent years, Beard was concerned about the fact that Thunderbird 1 took off so close to the Tracy house. Whereas the Space Shuttle launch pad is some four miles from the control centre, Thunderbird 1 lifts off just a few feet from the main building – surely it would melt the windows?

Keen to maintain the overall aesthetic but make the launch slightly more realistic, Beard introduced a second swimming pool. While a small diving pool would sit slightly closer to the house, a second pool, somewhat larger and further from the house, would be located next to it. When the launch sequence was initiated, the bottom of the diving pool would rise up – the water pouring over the sides – and the main pool would begin sliding underneath both it and the Tracy house.

A similar issue of realism arose for the round house, or library as it was now called, through which Thunderbird 3 passed during its launch. The eventual concept for the library was inspired by Brazilian architect Oscar Niemeyer's Museum of Contemporary Art in Niteroi, Brazil. Ninety-seven-year-old Oscar Niemeyer has created some 500 different buildings. Inspired by his homeland's beaches, hills and women, Niemeyer's sensual style has been a hallmark of some of Brazil's most striking structures.

The country's capital, Brasilia – which was constructed over just four years in the 1950s – is branded throughout by Niemeyer's distinctive hand. In places, the city resembles the set of a science fiction movie from the 1930s, so it is perhaps not surprising that Niemeyer's work should be the inspiration

for John Beard's re-imagining of the Tracy Island library.

There was just one problem: when the library design was scaled up it turned out to be too small for Thunderbird 3 to squeeze through. Although the library could be expanded it would have to hold an awful lot of books if it was going to be big enough. It was for this reason that it was decided to split the library in three. This seemed to fit with the outrageous nature of the rest of the island.

With the library, the island's crowning glory, completed, the Tracys' home had both shape and form.

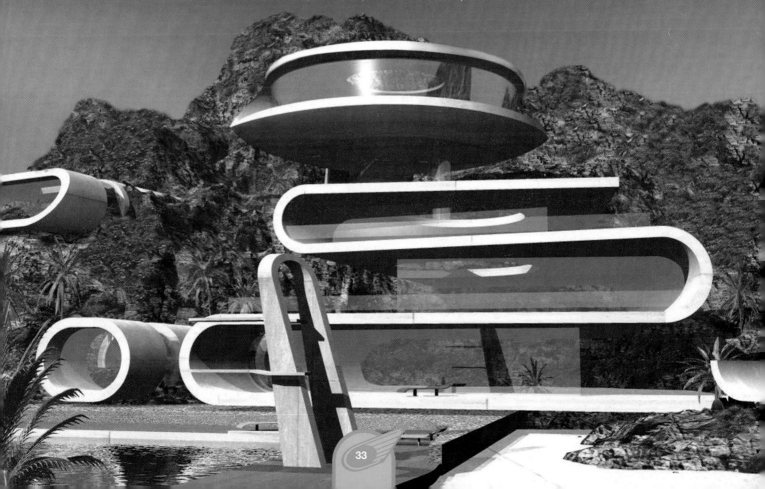

DESIGNING THUNDERBIRD 1

The design for Thunderbird 1, the spearhead vessel in the International Rescue fleet, went through more changes than any other vehicle.

The initial design was harder, and looked more menacing, than the ship from the original series. Despite this, that particular concept drawing developed quite a long way before the decision was taken to steer away from such military looks. Instead, the team began work on a design that was a little more fun.

Although a few other variations arose – in one the ship looked very much like the Lockheed Starfighter of the 1950s, while other ideas were inspired by 1950s rockets – the design gradually began to develop into a look that was similar to the model that appeared in the series.

This design underwent considerable refinement. For one thing, the engines were made bigger in order to reflect the craft's enormous speed and power, while some of the side thrusters were designed to swing down upon landing (curiously, this was one of the few design ideas from the 1997 production to be included in the movie).

There was also some debate about the craft's wings. The original Thunderbird 1 had a swing wing that swept back when it was travelling at high speed, but spread out when the ship was travelling slowly or coming in to land. After toying with a few variations, the team decided that they should stick with the original.

Perhaps the most significant departure from the television series came with the decision to make the cockpit transparent. This being a live action motion picture it was important for the pilot to be visible. As you might expect, once this decision had been made, the team still had to decide where the cockpit was going to go – should the pilot, Scott, be visible from the bottom and the top, or simply from above?

This wasn't the only major departure from the original design. The demands of the story were such that, at one point, Thunderbird 1 was going to have to transport three passengers. This being the case, the crew area also had to expand considerably, although it was decided that the cockpit canopy would not be extended backwards to make everyone on the craft visible.

TB1 cockpit

Thunderbird 1
© Levery 2000

Pilots harness

FROM CONCEPT TO COMPUTER

Once the final design for Thunderbird 1 had been completed by the concept artist, and the blueprints drawn up by the art director, the designs were passed on to the modelling team at Framestore CFC. John Beard had agreed that he too would like to collaborate with Framestore CFC, and it was time to start putting this relationship to the test.

In many ways, the process of creating a model on a computer is very much like sculpting or moulding clay. The modellers start with a primitive shape, a sphere or a cube, that is represented by a series of wires – it is for this reason that the computer models they create are often called wireframes.

Starting with this primitive shape, the modeller begins stretching it and widening it, adding extra shapes, until the wireframe begins to resemble the concept artist's sketches. As they did this, the modellers often noticed that certain angles were missing, or that aspects needed to be detailed further. The close relationship that was developing between modellers and designers meant that they didn't just have to guess what these details were supposed to be – the modellers could actually ask the concept artist to flesh them out.

The benefits of the relationship also became apparent once the initial computer model was complete. At this point, John Beard was able to review the wireframe model on a virtual turntable. This gave him the opportunity to see which aspects didn't quite work, and what needed to be tweaked or enhanced to make the final design succesful.

With the wireframe completed, the Framestore CFC modellers were in a position to undertake shader work. If modelling is a bit like

creating a plastic model kit, this was the point when they began to put paint on the model – effectively to wrap a 'skin' around the wireframe and to begin giving that skin some texture.

There was a second stage to this process as well. Just as a model kit is made up of a number of different materials, so all the vehicles were to comprise a range of substances. Since everything reflects light in different ways, it was important to tell the computer how each part of the vessel would look when illuminated. The result was a richness and depth to the crafts' overall appearance.

Thunderbird 1 was in many ways a test case, but the successful interaction between the 3D modellers and John Beard's design team was already demonstrating that the decision to ask the two groups to work together was paying off.

PROFILECRAIG LYN – CG SUPERVISOR

Craig Lyn joined Framestore CFC to work on *Dinotopia* and then *Harry Potter and the Chamber of Secrets* (2002). Prior to that he had worked on such films as *Pearl Harbor* (2001), *Mission to Mars* (2000), and *The Phantom Menace* (1999).

Lyn's main responsibility on *Thunderbirds* has been overseeing the modelling and animating of the vehicles. He was also involved during pre-production in the pre-visualisation and animatics work.

Lyn describes the animatics as 'brainstorming in 3D': 'We have to be prepared to take an idea, run with it, and throw it away the next day.'

DESIGNING THUNDERBIRD 2

Dominic Lavery did much of the initial concept work on Thunderbird 2: 'It's arguably everyone's favourite Thunderbird,' he says. 'It felt sort of sacrilegious: I was sat there redesigning this thing that not only me but lots of other people love.' Because of the affection with which Thunderbird 2 is held, the design team went out of their way to keep the new version of the ship looking like the original.

As with Thunderbird 1, however, there was an effort to make the workhorse of the Thunderbird fleet longer, sleeker and cleaner. It was for this reason that it was decided to remove the engines that were attached to the rear wing of the original vehicle.

One of the team's other concerns was the fact that this huge, heavy aircraft was so preposterous. Thunderbird 2 couldn't possibly fly – especially when it only has two little wings on either side. To address this, they turned to drawings of the American B2 Stealth Bomber and the Flying Wing aircraft of World War II. Inspired by these planes they attempted to create a hard edge around the middle seam of the craft which would give a sense that Thunderbird 2 was also a kind of flying wing. They felt that only by doing this could they ground the vessel in some kind of reality.

PODS

Reviewing episodes of the original series, John Beard had noticed that the size of Thunderbird 2 would sometimes change massively throughout the course of a story. Although when it arrived at a rescue situation it would drop pods that were as big as an aircraft hangar, when it took off from Tracy Island, Thunderbird 2 was about half the size of the palm trees, 'The change in scale seemed to be about 500 per cent,' he says.

Since the film was going to include real actors, it would be harder to get away with these drastic variations, so they decided to go with a Thunderbird 2 that was at the larger end of the scale.

A second concern was the fact that the vehicles inside the pods seemed to be tiny in comparison. It seemed absurd that Thunderbird 2 would travel all the way to a disaster, carrying just one small vehicle, when there was a chance that other equipment might also be required.

All of these considerations led to a radical rethink of Thunderbird 2's pods. Instead of having six distinct pods, each containing different equipment, there would be no such thing as a full pod. Instead, each vehicle would be housed in a pod segment. Thunderbird 4 would be contained in a segment half the size of a pod, for example, while the Thunderizer and the Firefly would each be stored in quarter-sized segments.

Although it isn't seen in the finished film, an idea developed that, when the alert sounded, appropriate segments would be combined to form a full pod. They would be

positioned under Thunderbird 2 and it would settle down over them. In this way, during the oil rig disaster the central segment of the pod housed the Rescue Platform. In contrast, during The Hood's journey to London, the pod was made up of three segments that housed Thunderbird 4 at the front, the Mole in one of the rear segments, and another vehicle – which we don't see – in the other rear segment.

In John Beard's eyes this radical revision made Thunderbird 2 a far more flexible vehicle. In effect, it had become a giant toolbox.

THE ISSUE OF THE LEGS

Aside from the overall look and size of the ship and the construction of its pods, there were a number of other aspects of Thunderbird 2 that needed resolving. In particular, John Beard had concerns about its legs.

Looking at the television series, Beard couldn't help but think that the legs of the original were somewhat flimsy, and couldn't possibly support the weight of something the size of this immense cargo vehicle.

There were a number of different designs for new legs. The design team considered introducing a peculiarly complex hydraulic lift, and even explored the possibility of including legs with wheels on – rather like those of an Antanov cargo plane. This idea was discarded when it was decided that there was insufficient space within Thunderbird 2's structure to stow such substantial undercarriage. It was ultimately decided that the ship would land on four, very powerful-looking, hydraulic legs.

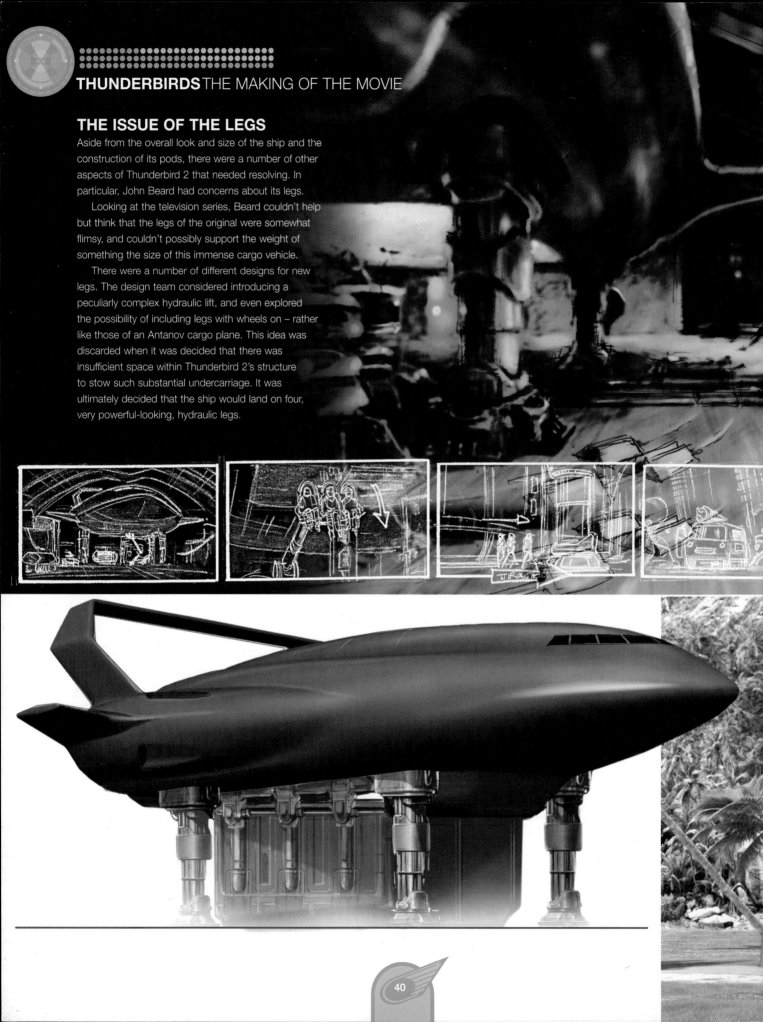

ENTER THE TRANSPORTER

Thunderbird 2's transporter is, in many ways, the design team's boldest departure from the original series. For most people, the launch of Thunderbird 2 – rolling out from the cliff, the palm trees collapsing on either side, the ramp lifting up – captures the whole magical essence of the original series. This was certainly true of the designers, and they were keen to pay tribute to that remarkable sequence.

In order to do this, a mechanism was required to transport Thunderbird 2 to its launchpad. The Transporter was just such a mechanism. Essentially a sled that would carry Thunderbird 2 into position, its design was inspired by pictures of sports utility vehicles that the designers had found in various car magazines. A combination of four wheel drives, estates, and sports cars, sports utility vehicles had just the look that Beard was trying to capture.

There was one problem, however: with the introduction of the redesigned pods, Thunderbird 2's launch sequence had become even more complicated. Now, the pod segments would be assembled on top of the Transporter, this would then slide back underneath Thunderbird 2 which would lower itself down, over the pod and onto the Transporter.

VEHICLE PROFILE

FIREFLY

The majority of International Rescue's operations involve fire-fighting of one form or another and the Firefly always plays a vital role in such disasters.

The Firefly boasts a large plough, enabling it to clear away rubble and get to the heart of a blaze. Once there the Firefly ejects nitro-glycerine shells to disperse the flames. Where this isn't appropriate, the vehicle's cannon can be used to spray water or foam into a fire. Alternatively, in forest fires, its tanks can be filled with sticky water; capable of adhering to the surface of trees, this glue-like water is good at limiting the damage caused by a blaze.

The Firefly isn't the only vehicle that International Rescue uses during fire-fighting operations: it also has a fire truck and tender that it can bring to bear.

ADAPTED BUCKET

CATERPILLAR STUDDED WHEELS

DESIGNING FIREFLY

Like the Mole and the Thunderizer, the Firefly was built for real. The wheels of the vehicle were relatively wide and it wasn't possible for the design team to find rubber tracks broad enough to fit over them. While they could have used standard caterpillar tracks, these would have torn up the stage floor and caused considerable damage.

Ray Chan was the art director working on the Firefly. His solution was to bolt rubber lorry stops onto the vehicle's steel wheels, to provide a tread-like effect and to cushion them.

In one scene, the Firefly is used to fire foam at Mullion and his henchmen. Chan helped facilitate this shot by removing one of the back doors of the Firefly, allowing the special effects team to set up their equipment in the space behind.

DESIGNING THUNDERBIRD 3

If Thunderbird 2 is a preposterous vehicle then Thunderbird 3 is almost as far-fetched – a huge rocket that takes off into the skies and then comes back down again, all in one piece.

In the early stages of the design a number of discussions took place about the possibility of introducing a little more realism into the vehicle. With the general public now familiar with how rockets discard sections as they travel into space, and aware of how the space shuttle ejects its booster rockets and fuel tank as it reaches orbit, the design team discussed the possibility of doing something similar with Thunderbird 3.

A number of variations were explored. In one, Thunderbird 3 would also discard its lower sections until the nose cone was undertaking the last part of the journey, docking with Thunderbird 5 and then returning back down to Tracy Island on its own.

An alternative suggestion was even more radical. In this variation, Thunderbird 3 would effectively be a giant booster rocket, piggy-backing a small shuttle into space, which would again do the last bit of the journey. Whether it would then return to Earth on its own, or on the back of Thunderbird 3, was never quite decided.

As the story developed and it became necessary for International Rescue's rocket to travel to London from Thunderbird 5, it was eventually decided to return to Gerry Anderson's original concept. A few minor variations on the final design were nevertheless attempted: some sketches excluded the struts connecting the engines to the main body, while air intakes on the engines themselves were introduced before being abandoned.

The most significant difference between this new, retro-modern, version of Thunderbird 3 and the original, were the landing rings that extend from the engines when the ship arrives in London.

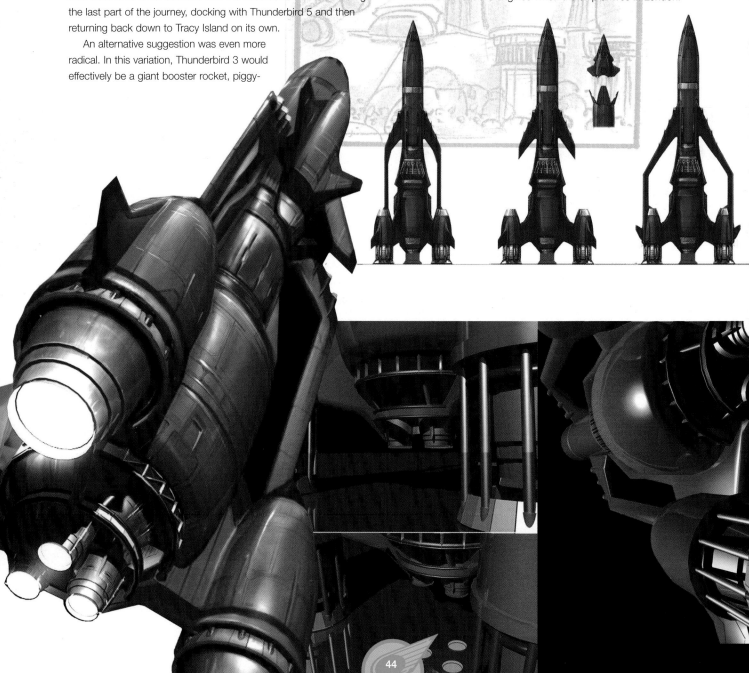

A QUESTION OF SCALE

Getting the scale right for all the vehicles was extremely tricky, as the design team had already seen with Thunderbird 2. 'I'd word out the basic proportions of a vehicle, scale the whole thing up, and then realise the pilot wouldn't fit inside!' says Dominic Lavery.

As we have already seen, Thunderbird 3 was even more of an issue: the designers had worked out how large it should be before realising that it wouldn't fit through the ringed library. Indeed, the library would have had to have been the size of the British Museum in order for the rocketship to get through the middle.

Once again, the collaboration with Framestore CFC helped the design team to find a solution. They were able to experiment with size and scale using Framestore CFC's wireframe models of the ship and library, rather than by developing repeated concept sketches.

The relationship was also proving to be beneficial in a quite separate way. On effects-heavy films, once designs are passed to an effects house modellers sometimes introduce new ideas that have not been approved by the production designer. On *Thunderbirds*, the creative urges of the effects staff were being channelled into the overall design process. This time, the final designs were going to be ones that the director had signed off on. The close relationship between Framestore CFC and the design team was definitely paying dividends.

REAL ROBOTS

Even the brilliant Brains was not capable of building a fleet of ultra-sophisticated craft and vehicles on his own. As a nod to this, a number of robots can be seen in the Thunderbird 2 silo. The implication is that much of the development and maintenance of the craft is carried out by these automatons.

Unusually for *Thunderbirds*, these robots weren't built for the movie, but hired from German robotics manufacturer Kuka. That said, the basic look and feel of the Kuka robots went on to be used for other elements of the design. The armatures that suspend Thunderbirds 1 and 3 in their silos are basically larger, more embellished versions of these robots. The same is the case with the mechanisms that open the main entrance to Thunderbird 2's silo during the launch sequence.

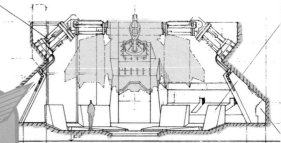

DESIGNING THUNDERBIRD 4

Unlike Thunderbird 3, International Rescue's underwater rescue vehicle underwent a considerable amount of change before the final design was agreed. In contrast to Thunderbirds 1, 2 and 3, Thunderbird 4 had not aged well. Furthermore, John Beard was concerned that, given that it was supposed to be used to save peoples' lives, the original vehicle was quite limited in its functionality, while its rather box-like appearance was uninspiring.

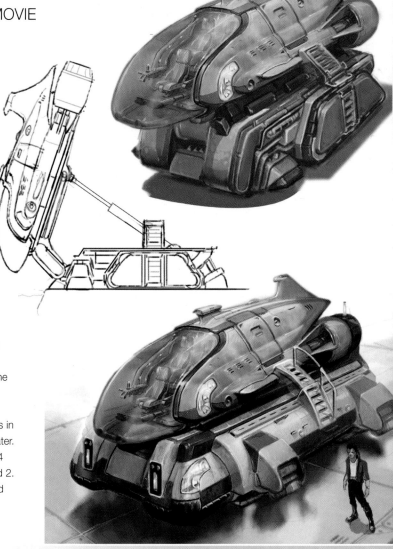

For these reasons, the design team set about creating a more user-friendly vehicle – more flexible and dynamic than the original Thunderbird 4. They wanted to produce a submersible that was as versatile underwater as its sister craft were in the air. Initially at least, the team also wanted a craft that was somewhat larger than the original, which was rather small in comparison to the other Thunderbirds.

Very quickly, this increased flexibility was realised by a pair of robotic arms that were folded up beneath the main cockpit but which would unfurl and extend when required. The designers also attempted to make the position of the airlock more obvious.

At one point in Thunderbird 4's development, the film's storyline required the ship to travel over ground. In response to this, a hoversled was sketched, upon which the diminutive submarine could sit and ride across both land and water. When the sled was in position, Thunderbird 4 could then slide off and slip under the water.

One of the great things about this sled was that Thunderbird 4 would be able to climb back onto it, and so return to Thunderbird 2. Thus, one of the many great mysteries of the original series would be answered.

Sadly, as the story evolved further, the need for this intriguing new aspect to Thunderbird 4 disappeared, and so the hoversled was similarly retired.

IMPROVING VISIBILITY

As with Thunderbird 1, Jonathan Frakes was very keen for the pilot of Thunderbird 4 to be far more visible. It was this requirement that had the greatest influence on early designs of the craft.

A number of variations were attempted. In one of these the craft had a spherical cockpit. Although very striking, the cost of realising this was prohibitive. Thunderbird 4 was going to have to be built for real, and the construction of a glass or Perspex dome would have been exorbitant.

The penultimate design for the submarine was perhaps the most intriguing of all. Moving away from the original drawings of Thunderbird 4 altogether, this idea consisted of a submersible whose lines broadly followed those of Thunderbird 2.

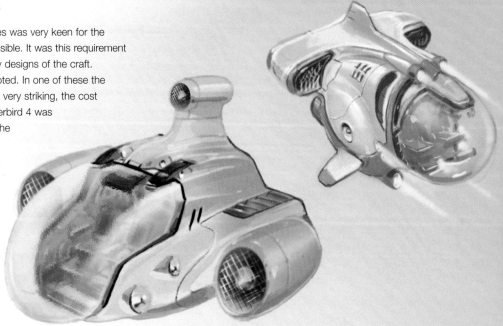

Although an innovative concept, Beard wanted a design that was closer to the original. This version initially stretched to some 35 feet in length. However, as it developed it gradually became more compact. Jonathan Frakes wanted to see Thunderbird 4 as 'the little engine that could' – he wanted it to be a pint-sized vessel that was far more powerful than it at first appeared.

Curiously, this disproportionate strength ended up having an impact on the design of the monorail, which features at the end of the film. During the movie's finale, Thunderbird 4 lifts one of the monorail carriages out of the Thames. In order to emphasise the unlikely power of the yellow submarine, the size of the monorail carriage was actually increased.

Of course, it wasn't just in size that the new Thunderbird 4 eventually came to resemble the original. As well as being yellow,

the submersible also boasts the same vertical fin at the back, as well as small fins on either side and the same tubular engines. The robotic arms remain, and there is much more glass, but the craft's relationship to Anderson's original vehicle can still be seen.

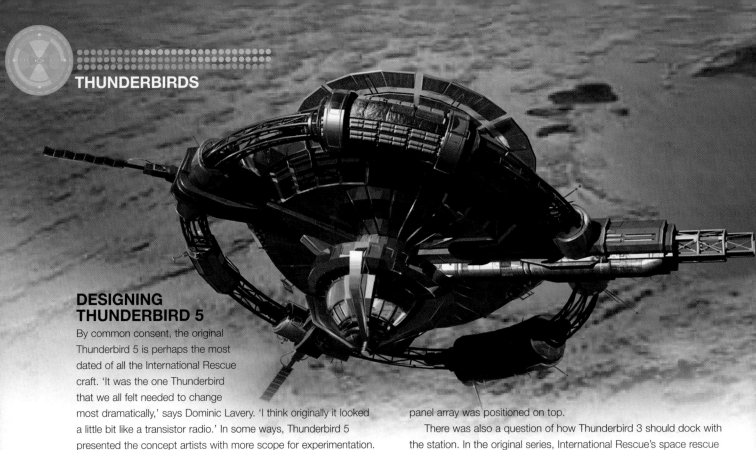

DESIGNING THUNDERBIRD 5

By common consent, the original Thunderbird 5 is perhaps the most dated of all the International Rescue craft. 'It was the one Thunderbird that we all felt needed to change most dramatically,' says Dominic Lavery. 'I think originally it looked a little bit like a transistor radio.' In some ways, Thunderbird 5 presented the concept artists with more scope for experimentation.

At the beginning of the design process, the concept artists spent a lot of time looking at the International Space Station, as well as designs for future space stations, images of contemporary satellites, and ideas from the interior of the Space Shuttle's cargo bay. Very often, the artists would simply look at small elements and details and magnify them.

Behind all of this research was a desire to create something with clean lines, and this led the design team to conceive Thunderbird 5 as a large, circular space station. Some early designs were described by Lavery as being very futuristic. In particular, one design resembled a large ring doughnut with a chunk bitten out of it. It was quickly decided that this idea was *too* futuristic, and too far-removed from the original Thunderbird 5.

The tubular ring that ran round the outside of the original space station was integrated into the new version, but the design and position of Thunderbird 5's solar panels changed radically. Initial drawings had the panels located in the familiar mirrors-on-sticks structure that hung beneath the station, but later, a circular solar panel array was positioned on top.

There was also a question of how Thunderbird 3 should dock with the station. In the original series, International Rescue's space rescue rocket connected with the station head on. The design team experimented with this before moving on to other ideas. One of these was of a large umbilical arm that would unfurl and lock onto the rocketship.

Finally, it was decided to introduce a permanent umbilicous that the side of Thunderbird 3 would connect to. As the space station was being designed, work on Thunderbird 3 hadn't even begun. For this reason, the actual docking mechanism was left undefined and some early concept art lacks this detail.

As with the other craft, colour was a definite concern. Again, to make a very definite link with the original series, a similar overall colour scheme was adopted. However, it was also decided to introduce new elements, integrating the gold-coloured foil that is often seen on contemporary satellites.

The designers also wanted to create a space station that was comfortable to live in. Whereas Mir and the ISS are notoriously cramped, Thunderbird 5 would be open and spacious, with an expansive control room and wide corridors.

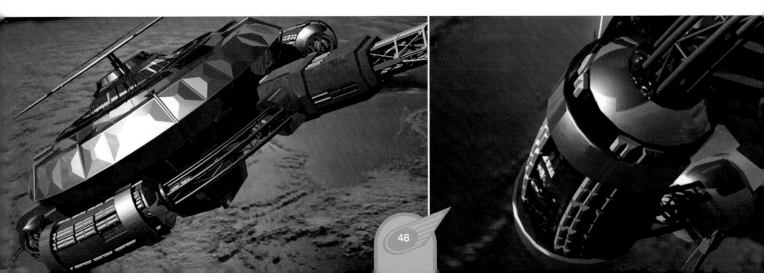

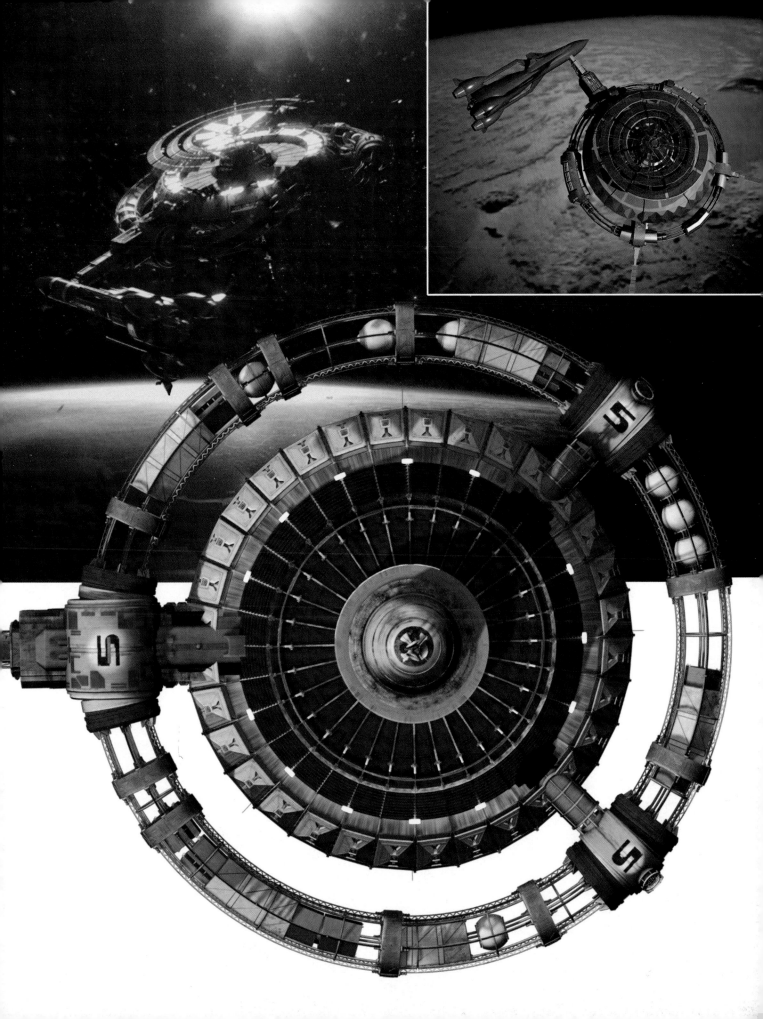

DESIGNING THE MONORAIL

Monorails come in a wide variety of designs, and the variation of concept sketches completed for the movie reflect this. Some monorails – such as the one in Seattle, Washington – run on top of a rail, and some sketches were made along these lines before the final design was agreed. This design depicted a passenger car that ran beneath the rail itself. It was felt that this design would be easier to realise, and would better fit the storyline – it would be hard to drop the monorail into the Thames if it had to fall off the rail first!

Sticklers for detail, Framestore CFC actually located the monorail on the route from Waterloo Station to Stratford in east London. Given that the new London athletics stadium is being built at Stratford, the route implies that London won the 2012 bid to host the Olympic Games.

PRE-VISUALISATION

As well as working alongside the production designer and contributing to the development of the film's overall look and feel, Framestore CFC were also given the job of pre-visualisation.

Through discussions with Jonathan Frakes and director of photography Brendan Galvin, artist John Greaves had identified which camera angles they were looking to use in each scene, and whether these shots would be close, middle distance, or far away. He then began translating the outcome of these discussions into a long series of pictures, or storyboards.

As the storyboards were delivered, Framestore CFC began the process of pre-visualisation. This involved taking Greaves' storyboards and animating them, making the figures move and recording dialogue over the top.

For the more involved effects sequences, Framestore CFC created animatics. Essentially, these are very basic computer animations in which the flow of the action can be captured. As with the storyboards, the animatics would indicate which camera angles were going to be used and how each shot would be framed. Once agreed by Frakes, these would then be the starting point for the development of the effects scenes proper.

The dream sequence which was originally going to open the movie was sketched out using animatics over just two or three days. Since so little time had been spent on the development of the sequence it didn't really matter when Frakes and the production team decided to abandon it. Some eight or nine sequences were ultimately developed using these animatics.

Pre-visualisation was invaluable in helping both Frakes and the producers to see how the movie was shaping up. By the time the actual shoot began, pre-visualisation had been completed for almost 70 per cent of the film.

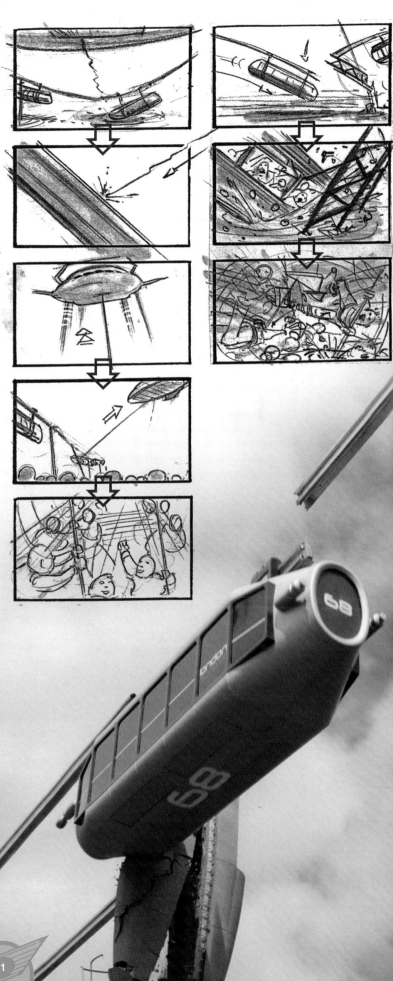

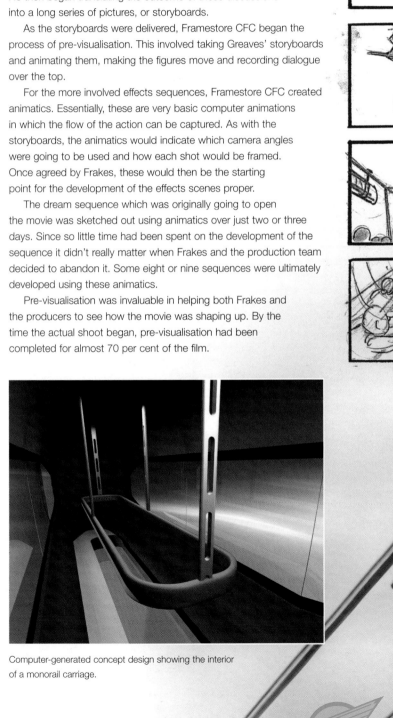

Computer-generated concept design showing the interior of a monorail carriage.

REELING IN THE BIG FISH

A cornerstone of Working Title's success is the belief in the need to make the bull's eye for the success of a film as large as possible. The larger the target, the easier it is to hit. Implicit in this philosophy is the requirement to attach big name actors to every production.

Thunderbirds was no exception. Although it was a children's film, it would be adults taking their children to see it. If some of the stars were familiar, then the movie would be a far more attractive prospect.

When Jonathan Frakes came on board it was not immediately apparent who should play the villain. In early drafts of the script, International Rescue's adversary was one Aristotle Spode. One of Frakes' key contributions to script discussions was the suggestion that they switch to The Hood. 'We collectively realised that there was no real advantage to introducing a new villain, when The Hood is a classic villain from the original show and is also a really wonderful, maniacal character,' says the director.

Once they had decided to go with The Hood as the villain, Sir Ben Kingsley became the obvious choice to take the role. 'Sir Ben had been doing some very heavy duty films, including *House of Sand and Fog* (2003), for which he's been nominated for an Oscar™, and he was also very keen to spend the summer in England,' says Tim Bevan, remembering his approach to the actor.

Enthusiastic about doing something that was a little less intense, and encouraged by his sons, Kingsley expressed an interest in getting involved.

In making this decision, it certainly didn't hurt that Kingsley and Frakes both shared mutual friends in Patrick Stewart. Frakes had starred alongside Stewart in *Star Trek: The Next Generation* since 1987, while Kingsley's association with the veteran actor went back much further, the pair having worked together at the Royal Shakespeare Company in the 1960s and 70s.

As soon as Frakes and Kingsley met, they got on extremely well. Frakes is amused to reflect on the fact that Kingsley is the second bald, British, Shakespearean actor he has worked with during his career.

FILLING JEFF TRACY'S SHOES

When discussions with Universal Studios began, Bill Paxton emerged as a clear favourite to play Jeff Tracy. Described by Tim Bevan as an 'all American Texan', Paxton is well known in the United States for his roles in films such as *Aliens* (1986), *Apollo 13* (1995) and *Titanic* (1997).

His wife being English, Paxton was that rare thing in America – a man who was already familiar with *Thunderbirds*. For this reason, the prospect of starring in the movie was highly attractive. This was fortunate for, as Bevan has admitted, 'I don't know

what we would have done if Paxton hadn't been available.'

With two of the four main adult roles now filled, the hunt was on for someone to take the role of Brains, the inventor of the Thunderbird vehicles, and Lady Penelope – International Rescue's glamorous London agent. Once again, fortune favoured the production and Anthony Edwards was cast to play Brains.

Edwards had heard about the film while talking with a friend who worked for Working Title in Los Angeles. Edwards is best known for having played the tragic Dr Greene in the medical drama *ER*. 'When we were told that we could get Anthony Edwards it became something of a no-brainer,' says Frakes. 'First of all he's a great actor, but secondly he's just huge as Dr Greene.'

The search for an actress to play Lady Penelope took a slightly different form. Although they auditioned a number of big name actresses for the role, in the end director and producers decided to go with the relatively unknown Sophia Myles. 'When Sophia tested, Mark Huffam and I looked at each other and we just knew that, because of her performance and her confident Lady Penelope air, we had found who we needed,' says Frakes.

CASTING PENELOPE

Looking back on her audition for Lady Penelope, Sophia Myles thinks it was an advantage that she didn't have any knowledge of the original series. Never having watched *Thunderbirds* as a child, she knew nothing about the role and nor did she have time to do any research. Working full time on another project, Myles simply read the script and went along to a meeting with Frakes.

BILL PAXTON

For Bill Paxton, *Thunderbirds* harks back to a less selfish, more altruistic age. 'When I grew up in the 1960s, life was about vocation. It wasn't about making money. It was about doing things for other people, finding something you wanted to do. There's a message of integrity and ethics all through this film. It celebrates technology as benefiting mankind, using these machines to try to actually help people, instead of decimating them.'

Seeing himself as a filmmaker rather than simply an actor, in 2003 Paxton directed and starred in *Frailty*, a story about a blue collar worker who, in the belief that he is avenging God, suddenly sets out on a killing spree. Paxton is also slated to direct *The Greatest Game Ever Played*, which is due to be released in 2005.

Paxton's two children and his wife – who hails from the UK – stayed with him throughout *Thunderbirds*' filming.

JEFF TRACY

The death of his wife forced billionaire ex-astronaut Jeff Tracy to face up to his responsibilities to his five sons and to humanity as a whole.

International Rescue was established as a response to this tragedy. Jeff wanted to prevent others from experiencing the kind of loss that he had suffered and he wanted to build something he could share with his sons.

Ironically, although International Rescue was to bring him closer to his children, it also forced him to put them in danger on an almost daily basis. The thought of losing one of his sons during a rescue operation was a constant anxiety to Jeff and an ongoing reminder of the losses he had already felt during his life.

Despite these pressures, Jeff's discipline and training allowed him to hide his worries from his sons. It was only during conversations with his eldest son John, and occasionally with Lady Penelope, that he allowed himself to reveal his concerns.

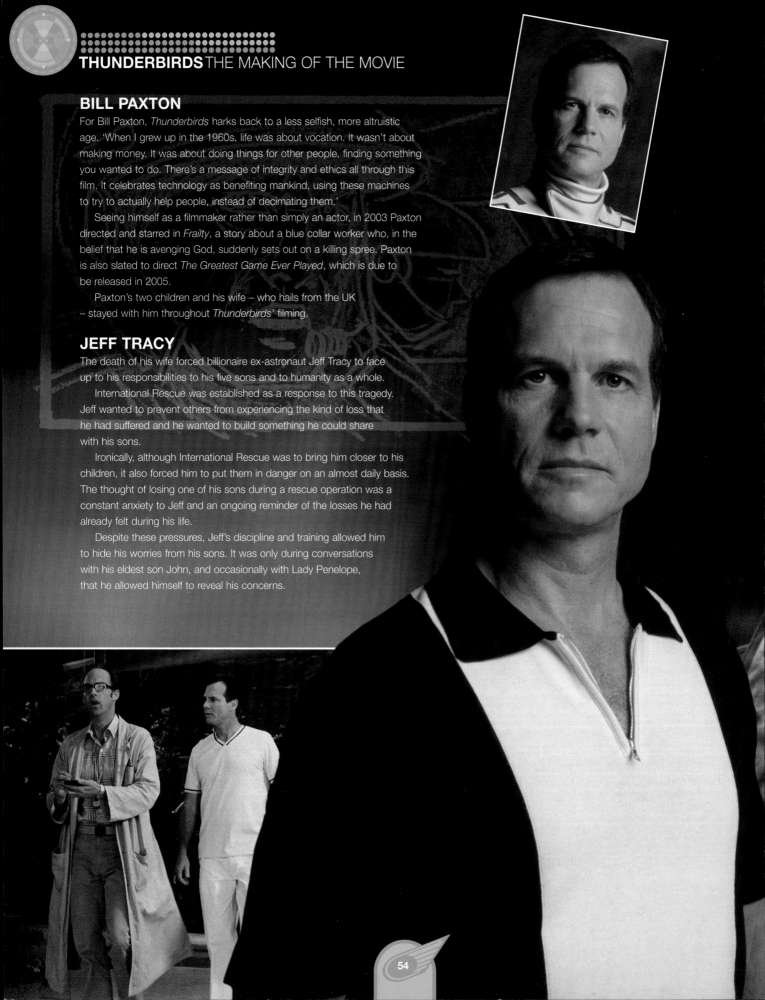

ANTHONY EDWARDS

Once he had decided to give the role of Brains to Anthony Edwards, Jonathan Frakes called the actor, leaving a message on his voicemail. Appropriately enough, when Edwards returned Frakes' call, the director was enjoying a meal at Green's Restaurant.

Made famous by his role as Dr Mark Greene in *ER*, Edwards left the long running series in 2002 after spending eight years in the part. An unassuming character actor with a dry wit, Edwards is still remembered fondly for his role as Goose in *Top Gun* (1986).

It was during his time in the cult series *Northern Exposure* that Edwards first gained critical attention. Cast as Mike Monroe, the allergy sufferer cum hypochondriac who lived in a giant plastic bubble, Edwards' portrayal of the eccentric recluse was utterly in keeping with the quirky nature of the series.

HYRAM 'BRAINS' HACKENBACKER

When Jeff Tracy invited the brilliant engineer Hyram 'Brains' Hackenbacker to help build International Rescue, he seized the opportunity. Although the work would be both rewarding and stimulating, Brains was also attracted by what it meant for his son. The prospect of raising him on a tropical island, alongside five other young boys, was extremely appealing.

Possessing one of the most brilliant minds in the world, Brains' stutter was not caused by nerves but by his ferocious intelligence. His brain moved so much faster than his mouth, his words were constantly tripping over and running into each other.

Over the following years, Brains' mind was to have something else to occupy it. Working in partnership with Jeff Tracy, Brains was to give form to Jeff's dream and bring his remarkable vision to life.

CASTING THE KIDS

The casting of the children was to be the only time in the *Thunderbirds* production that Jonathan Frakes was to work with a familiar face. Mary Gail Artz and Barbara Cohen had both worked on the casting of several John Boorman films, including *Beyond Rangoon* (1995) and *The Tailor of Panama* (2001), as well as a number of Disney films. They had also worked with Frakes on the casting of *Clockstoppers*.

In total, Artz and Cohen auditioned some 8,000 children for the parts of Alan, Tin-Tin and Fermat. At the end of each week they would send a tape to Frakes to review and then they would discuss what they had seen and agree who to move onto the next stage.

Eventually, in a single weekend in October 2002, a workshop was held in the US. On the Saturday, 60 children were invited along. 'We played theatre games, played scenes from the film, talked to them,' says Frakes, 'and by the end of the first day we had narrowed the choice down to 20 individuals.'

Sunday was a repeat of the day before, but as well as repeating those theatre games, they began mixing and matching different Alans with different Fermats, different Alans with different Tin-Tins, and different trios of actors together. 'Eventually we came down to two choices for Alan and the others,' says Frakes, 'and then it became clear that both individually and collectively, Brady, Soren and Vanessa were the team. They just worked well together.'

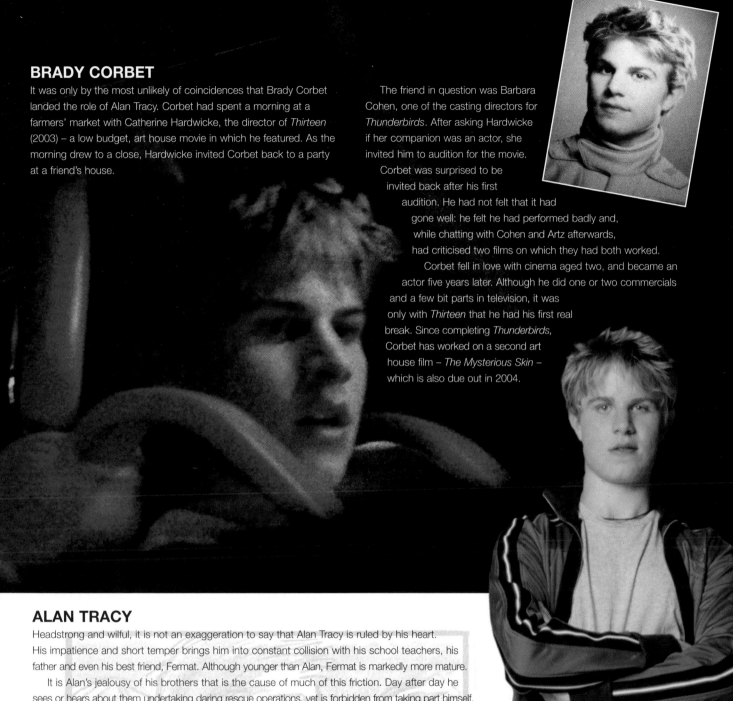

BRADY CORBET

It was only by the most unlikely of coincidences that Brady Corbet landed the role of Alan Tracy. Corbet had spent a morning at a farmers' market with Catherine Hardwicke, the director of *Thirteen* (2003) – a low budget, art house movie in which he featured. As the morning drew to a close, Hardwicke invited Corbet back to a party at a friend's house.

The friend in question was Barbara Cohen, one of the casting directors for *Thunderbirds*. After asking Hardwicke if her companion was an actor, she invited him to audition for the movie. Corbet was surprised to be invited back after his first audition. He had not felt that it had gone well: he felt he had performed badly and, while chatting with Cohen and Artz afterwards, had criticised two films on which they had both worked.

Corbet fell in love with cinema aged two, and became an actor five years later. Although he did one or two commercials and a few bit parts in television, it was only with *Thirteen* that he had his first real break. Since completing *Thunderbirds,* Corbet has worked on a second art house film – *The Mysterious Skin* – which is also due out in 2004.

ALAN TRACY

Headstrong and wilful, it is not an exaggeration to say that Alan Tracy is ruled by his heart. His impatience and short temper brings him into constant collision with his school teachers, his father and even his best friend, Fermat. Although younger than Alan, Fermat is markedly more mature.

It is Alan's jealousy of his brothers that is the cause of much of this friction. Day after day he sees or hears about them undertaking daring rescue operations, yet is forbidden from taking part himself.

However, behind the anger and resentment there is a young man who has the courage to admit when he is wrong, and who has a remarkable loyalty to his friends and family. As soon as he sees that his family is in trouble, Alan risks his life to rescue them, and when he causes upset to his friends he immediately apologies.

Alan's relationship with Tin-Tin undergoes an important change during The Hood's attack. Although they have grown up together, the pair have spent their childhood arguing and bickering with each other. It is only as they work together to defeat International Rescue's arch-enemy that they begin to draw closer to each other. Gradually, they realise that they only argue because they share a deeper bond.

Slowly, as Alan finally proves what he is capable of, some of his harder edges begin to soften. As he earns the respect of his family and his father he begins to show what kind of man he is to become.

VEHICLE PROFILE

THE MOLE

Sometimes, the only way to get to a disaster zone is underground. Thunderbird 2 can get you so far, but after that survivors can only be reached by burrowing through the rock and earth. It is at these times that International Rescue use their tunnelling machine, the appropriately named 'Mole'.

Boasting an innovative boring mechanism that allows it to grind through rock, stone and soil at unbelievable speeds, the Mole is ideal for reaching the survivors of mining disasters or even penetrating the rubble of fallen buildings.

What's more, the Mole's sophisticated sensors allow it to detect obstacles that might be in its path. When used in major cities with complex and labyrinthine infrastructures, these sensors are vital if the Mole is to avoid hitting a major power line, a sewer or even an underground railway. Unfortunately, The Hood had no qualms about doing this. During his attempt to break into the Bank of London he simply ploughed the Mole through one of the pylons supporting the London Monorail.

COSTUMES

For most of the movie's visual appearance, the designers made a special effort to update the original series for the new millennium. It was felt that this could not be achieved with the original *Thunderbirds* costumes. The blue pressed uniforms, sashes and hats were regarded as being too staid.

In discussions with costume designer Marit Allen, Frakes brought his own experience of space suits to bear. He wanted to see something form-fitting but not too tight – Frakes had spent seven years on *Star Trek: The Next Generation* having his modesty compromised by skin-tight costumes and he was unwilling to impose that on the cast of *Thunderbirds*.

Ultimately, Allen was inspired by the Steve McQueen driving uniform from the film *Le Mans* (1971). These half-turtleneck, silver overalls, with full turtlenecks underneath, captured the retro-modern gestalt that was being defined by John Beard and his team.

Taking these costumes one stage further, Allen also added different coloured trims. These were to vary depending on the individual. The pilot of Thunderbird 1 – Scott for the most part – would have a blue trim; Thunderbird 2's pilot would have green trim; red for Thunderbird 3; yellow for 4; and gold for Thunderbird 5.

PRETTY IN PINK

Marit Allen took an obvious steer from the original television series when she designed Lady Penelope's wardrobe – all the clothes had to be pink! Curiously, Allen didn't find this at all limiting: 'Once I began to dig and delve, there were so many different fabrics in pink and shades of pink and combinations of pink and soft yellow and soft lime green, it didn't seem restrictive at all.'

Allen was keen to give Penelope's clothes a retro influence, yet also to make them fashionable and specific to Penelope as an individual: 'There's a humorous smile in the direction of the 1960s, but hopefully they also look like the kind of things Lady Penelope would have chosen for herself if she were a real person,' she says.

VISITING BUCKINGHAM PALACE

The scene in which Lady Penelope is seen leaving Buckingham Palace wasn't in the original script, and came as something of a surprise to Marit Allen and her team. Having picked up an interesting, pom-pom-type fabric during a visit to Los Angeles, Allen decided to turn it into 'an amazing little cardigan coat with a hood' based on a pattern, again from the 1960s, which she had to hand.

▲ FLIGHT-SUIT IN PINK
For the journey to London in Thunderbird 1, Lady Penelope changes once again, this time into a pink version of the flight suit, with a special pink trim. She also wears a tailor-made Alice band with built-in earphone and mouthpiece.

◀ BATTLING THE HOOD

For her battle with The Hood and his minions, Lady P changes into a Capri-style outfit. 'This was the kind of thing a glamorous socialite would have worn when having Brandy Alexanders at sunset in Capri in Italy, in the 1960s,' remarks Allen. At that time, Capri was the fashionable destination for members of the international set who used to travel there for 'special weekends'. The island of Capri came to lend its name to this peculiar style of clothing with its three-quarter length trousers and sleeves and delicate sequin cuffs. In Lady Penelope's case, these sequins were mounted on a net to make them extremely light and provide the movement and flexibility needed during the fight sequence.

▶ PARTY ON

The pool-side celebration at the end of the film calls for Lady Penelope to wear what Allen describes as a Hawaiian sarong. Allen regards this as a glamorous, Hollywood version of a south sea island costume: 'It was inspired by the *Road to…* movies – *Road to Morocco*, *Road to Rio* and so on – starring Dorothy Lamour and Bing Crosby. Lamour invariably wore clothes like this in those movies.'

FINAL SHOWDOWN ▼

Always wear the right dress for the job: about to confront The Hood at the Bank of London, Lady Penelope slips into the costume Marit Allen regards as her favourite. The most distinctive element of this is the Organza coat which, for Allen, recalls the kinds of clothes that Grace Kelly used to wear during the 1960s, although Allen wasn't thinking of a particular film when she began sketching the design. 'I didn't go and look for a specific actress from a specific movie from the '60s that would work with a specific scene. Instead, the overall look of each outfit was a general nod to people that were great at that time.'

PROFILE MARIT ALLEN – COSTUME DESIGNER

Marit Allen's early career was a perfect grounding for her role on *Thunderbirds*. As fashion editor for the British *Vogue* magazine in the early 1960s she became an expert in the fashions of that period. Allen's move into film was the result of an invitation by her friend, the director Nicolas Roeg, who asked her to design costumes for his 1973 movie *Don't Look Now*. Her work with Roeg led to contributions to such diverse movies as Frank Oz's *Little Shop of Horrors* (1986), Stanley Kubrick's *Eyes Wide Shut* (1999) and Ang Lee's *Hulk* (2003).

FINDING TRACY ISLAND

Although work on the film's design and storyboards was progressing well, and the cast were beginning to fall into place, there remained one major area of uncertainty. This was the question of how Tracy Island was to be realised.

Early drafts of the script would have required up to six weeks of location shooting, and for a time South Africa appeared to have the right mix of locations. However, as the script continued to develop this shooting requirement reduced to just two weeks, while upon further investigation South Africa was beginning to look less and less suitable: the beaches were not white enough, the sea not blue enough, and the house that had identified as a possibility for the Tracy's home didn't seem quite right.

In response, Mark Huffam, John Beard and Jonathan Frakes began a broader location search. They looked again at South Africa, but also at Lord Howe Island, some 375 miles off the coast of Australia. Although they were immediately taken with it, problems soon began to emerge – there were too few palm trees for one thing, and although they could do some general aerial shots of the island it was really too isolated for actual location shooting. It was at this point that the team decided to turn their attention to the Seychelles, a cluster of small islands in the Indian Ocean. Flying around this breathtaking archipelago it became obvious that three or four of the islands were potentially suitable. North Island was ultimately selected.

Aloha from tracy Island

THE SEYCHELLES

Located just south of the equator, some would describe the climate of the Seychelles as favourable, while others would call it uncomfortably hot. Comprising an archipelago of 115 islands, the Seychelles can be found 1,000 miles east of Africa, and about 1,700 miles south-west of India.

Although some 76 of these islands are described as 'coral', meaning that they have literally grown out of the sea, the remainder are granitic. Many are simply rocky mountains that jut violently out of the sea and rise to heights of up to 1,000 metres.

North Island is one such specimen. While colonisation of the Seychelles only began in the eighteenth century, North Island remained uninhabited until very recently, when a luxurious holiday resort was established.

The most northern of the Seychelles' inner granitic islands, this mountainous little island perfectly embodied Tracy Island's beauty. Settling down to land in their helicopter after completing their recce, the relief was palpable for all three men. As he stepped out of the helicopter, Frakes proclaimed: 'We have found Tracy Island.'

They might have finally found their island, but there was still some debate about how the Tracys' house was going to be achieved. Should sets for the house be built in the Seychelles themselves? Or should they be constructed back at Pinewood Studios, where the bulk of the shoot was going to be conducted?

It quickly became clear that building in the Seychelles would be impossible, as the islands lack the infrastructure required to undertake such a major project. Another alternative was to build the set on the Pinewood lot and hope for a good summer. Unfortunately, for a June shoot, this would mean starting construction in March when British weather could be inclement. It soon became clear that constructing the set on one of Pinewood's stages was really the only option.

The final decision that needed to be made was how the exteriors of the Tracy house should be realised. There was the possibility of creating model miniatures and grafting these onto shots of the island, but Frakes quickly put paid to that idea: 'As technology moves forward, models find themselves in the dust,' he says. 'In general, model builds are really dangerous, really limited with regard to how you move the camera around. You either have the real thing and move the camera around it, or you have it fully CGI.'

There was another consideration as well. The Tracy house included a swimming pool, and making water work on miniature models is extremely difficult. With that taken into account as well, CGI was chosen as the most practical option.

LOCATING THE TRACY HOUSE

Even after the design team had obtained their pictures of the island there was some debate over where on the island the Tracy house was to be located. A number of variations were attempted. In one of these the house was to be positioned in the middle of the island, embedded into the hillside with the jungle on all sides.

Ultimately, the team decided not to go with this but positioned the house up the spine of a rocky outcrop at one end of the island. To do this, sections of the outcrop had to be gouged out by the computer modellers in order for the compound, with its various buildings and swimming pools, to sit comfortably in place.

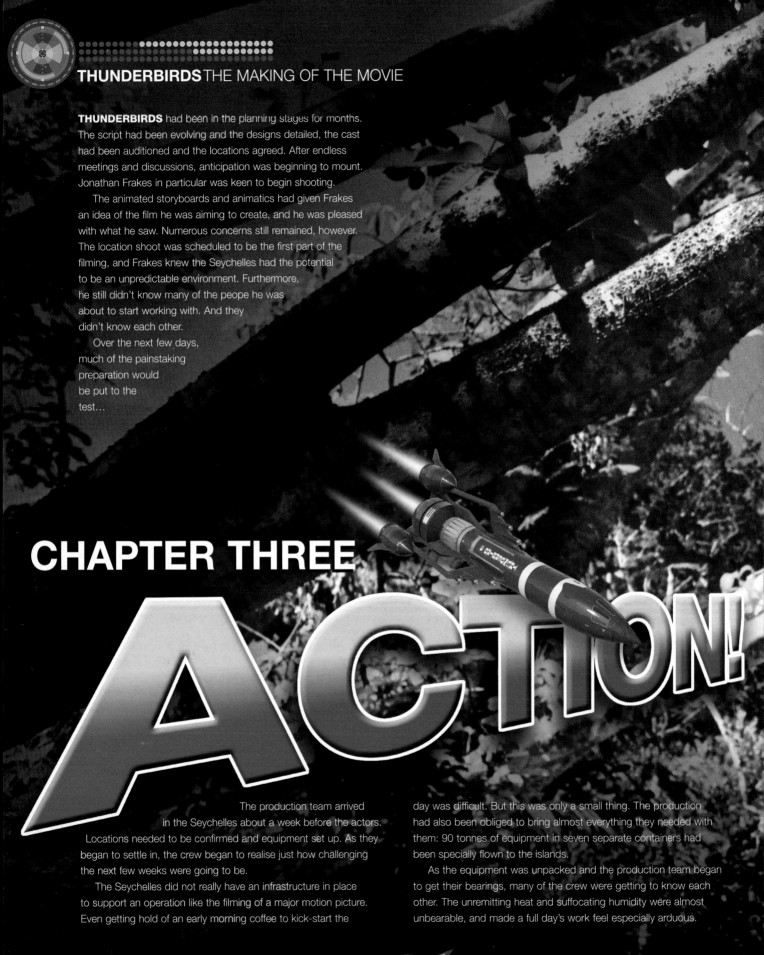

THUNDERBIRDS had been in the planning stages for months. The script had been evolving and the designs detailed, the cast had been auditioned and the locations agreed. After endless meetings and discussions, anticipation was beginning to mount. Jonathan Frakes in particular was keen to begin shooting.

The animated storyboards and animatics had given Frakes an idea of the film he was aiming to create, and he was pleased with what he saw. Numerous concerns still remained, however. The location shoot was scheduled to be the first part of the filming, and Frakes knew the Seychelles had the potential to be an unpredictable environment. Furthermore, he still didn't know many of the peope he was about to start working with. And they didn't know each other.

Over the next few days, much of the painstaking preparation would be put to the test…

CHAPTER THREE
ACTION!

The production team arrived in the Seychelles about a week before the actors. Locations needed to be confirmed and equipment set up. As they began to settle in, the crew began to realise just how challenging the next few weeks were going to be.

The Seychelles did not really have an infrastructure in place to support an operation like the filming of a major motion picture. Even getting hold of an early morning coffee to kick-start the day was difficult. But this was only a small thing. The production had also been obliged to bring almost everything they needed with them: 90 tonnes of equipment in seven separate containers had been specially flown to the islands.

As the equipment was unpacked and the production team began to get their bearings, many of the crew were getting to know each other. The unremitting heat and suffocating humidity were almost unbearable, and made a full day's work feel especially arduous.

Wish you were here!
Tracy Island

THUNDERBIRDS

SCENE 119 SLATE 131 TAKE 4

DIR: JONATHAN FRAKES
DOP: BRENDAN GALVIN
DATE 18 March 2003 ROLL:

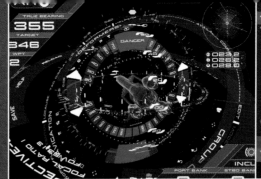

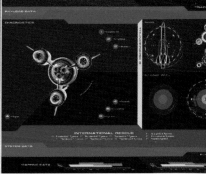

VEHICLE PROFILE

THUNDERBIRD 3

The design of Thunderbird 3 is nothing short of revolutionary. Whereas all contemporary space-going craft dispose of their fuel tanks as they climb into the atmosphere, Thunderbird 3 launches at such an incredible speed, and its hull is made of such a light alloy, that it is able to remain intact throughout every journey to and from space. This is just as well: having to build a new rocket for each launch of Thunderbird 3 would stretch even the resources of Jeff Tracy.

Thunderbird 3's main function in the International Rescue fleet is to effect crew exchange at Thunderbird 5 and to transport supplies and spare parts up to the space station.

From time to time, Thunderbird 3 is also involved in space-based rescue missions. As the International Space Station begins to age or satellites career out of control, it is sometimes down to International Rescue to intervene. Able to respond more quickly and effectively than other, more sluggish, space agencies, they are often better placed to embark on rescue operations.

What is arguably the most remarkable feature of Thunderbird 3 is its ability to land vertically. This is realised with the same anti-gravity engines that allow Thunderbirds 1 and 2 to take-off from disaster zones. Without this equipment it would not have been possible for International Rescue's giant red rocket to land in London's Jubilee Gardens, while returning to its silo on Tracy Island would also have been difficult.

Although it can be flown by just two people, it is usual for Thunderbird 3 to be manned by three of the Tracys. While Gordon and Virgil operate the control boards, it is left to Jeff to direct activities from his command chair.

Further to its crew, Thunderbird 3 is equipped to transport at least two passengers together with a significant amount of cargo. Thunderbird 5 needs to be resupplied on a regular basis while it also requires ongoing maintenance work. For this reason, spare parts and tools are a constant feature on Thunderbird 3's manifest.

ENGINES

As is the case with Thunderbird 1, most of Thunderbird 3's power is derived from its central engine. The three lateral engines provide additional thrust and serve to control pitch and yaw.

COCKPIT

Flying a rocket is not a one-man job and Thunderbird 3 is designed for a minimum crew of 2. Most often it is Virgil and Gordon who serve as pilots with their father, Jeff, directing operations from a centre seat, just behind their stations. Long experience as a NASA astronaut has more than qualified Jeff to train his sons and he sees his role on Thunderbird 3 as being to hone their piloting skills.

ENGINE STRUTS

They might appear superficial, but the three engine struts serve vital functions, carrying fuel to the engines and bearing the anti-gravity field lines that enable the ship to land vertically. Of course, given the speeds at which Thunderbird 3 is often forced to travel, these struts come under an incredible amount of stress. If it wasn't for them being forged from Brains' new, highly tensile, metal alloy, they would not be able survive a single launch.

LANDING RINGS

When coming in to land at Jubilee Gardens, landing rings extend from each of the lateral engines. The engines themselves are not strong enough to bear the weight of the entire craft and nor would Thunderbird 3 be able to balance on them effectively. The landing rings are therefore a vital feature of the ship's design.

SPECIFICATIONS

LENGTH: 175 feet
WINGSPAN: 23 feet
WEIGHT: 562 tons
MAXIMUM SPEED: 5,000 mph
RECOMMENDED CREW: 3
PASSENGERS: 3

SHOOTING THE SEYCHELLES

Although North Island had been chosen to represent the home of the Tracys, until recently it had been uninhabited. It is only in the last couple of years that a small holiday resort has been established there. For this reason, it was decided to base the production on a nearby, slightly larger, island. While aerial shots of North Island would be done, it was agreed that its neighbour provided the team with more flexibility.

Frustratingly, the first few days filming met with overcast skies and generally dismal weather. Extremely unusual for the Seychelles at that time of year, this began to place the schedule in some jeopardy. Later on in the shoot the crew managed to reshoot one of those days, but that was only through careful and meticulous planning.

As the filming continued, the relentless heat caused problems. The jungle sequences were particularly difficult. With the humidity even higher under the thick canopy, crew and cast alike began suffering from sprained ankles, cuts, scratches and insect bites.

To add to these difficulties, when planning each take, they had to ensure that no cocoa-de-mer palm trees would be captured in the frame. Native only to the Seychelles, the design team would not be able to include this plant on the set at Pinewood.

SETTLING IN

Although most of the cast had already met during the two week rehearsal period, it was the visit to the Seychelles that really allowed them to get to know each other.

For Ron Cook and Sophia Myles, this bonding took place during the long journey from the UK to the islands. Travelling together, they spent the entire journey talking and exchanging stories.

Upon his arrival, Cook learned that he had been billeted in a cabin on the beach, just a few feet away from the sea. He spent much of his first night sitting on the cabin's veranda, talking to Brady Corbet.

There was not one member of the production team who was not suffering from the heat. It was almost impossible for them to drink enough water or to replace the salt they were losing through their sweat.

Filming took place for six days a week, for as long as there was light available – and the sun stayed up for a very long time. Dressed in Parker's chauffeur uniform, Ron Cook found it especially uncomfortable in the sweltering climate.

In a sequence that never made it to the movie, FAB 1 – having transformed from a plane into a hydrofoil – is destroyed by one of The Hood's torpedoes. Parker and Penelope are forced to abandon ship and take to their escape vehicle: a pink pedalo. Parker, in his formal chauffeur's uniform, is seen driving and pedalling the vehicle to the shore as Penelope lounges behind him, resting beneath her pink parasol.

Professional to the last, Ron Cook pedalled furiously while a helicopter flew overhead for take after take. It was only at the end that Sophia Myles realised how draining it had been for him.

Of course, it wasn't all bad for Ron Cook. He and Sophia had been flown out early in order to get acclimatised, and shortly after shooting the sequence he learned he would have to stay in the Seychelles for a few more days.

The reason for the extended stay was simple: isolated as the Seychelles were, it was taking several days for the rushes of each day's filming

SIGHT-SEEING

The Seychelles might be paradise on earth, but there really isn't a great deal to do there. Nevertheless, as they waited to be called before the camera, the cast managed to keep themselves entertained.

For the younger cast members, there was less time to expend on leisure activities. They were far more involved in filming and they had to keep up with school work. The older actors, such as Ron Cook and Sophia Myles, had more time to spare and spent it visiting other islands, exploring the jungle, and snorkling.

To Cook's frustration he wasn't able to pursue his favourite past-time of diving because it was against the insurance rules. Similarly, Myles had been told not to get caught by the sun – she had to maintain her pale complexion. What everyone in the cast did manage to do was sample the local delicacy of fruitbat!

to be processed by the laboratory, and the production team wanted to be certain that Cook and Myles' pedalo sequence had worked. If necessary, the sequence might have to be filmed a second time.

On top of the unbearable weather, and the need to get all his shots right, Jonathan Frakes had additional concerns. With cast and crew coming together for the first time, he was aware that the location filming could make or break the whole team. For this reason, everyone was encouraged to eat together in the evenings, while every night he wandered round the resort, checking that everyone was happy and comfortable. This diligence added to the general *bon homie*.

As the shoot drew to a close, it became apparent that, despite the pressures they were under, a team spirit was beginning to develop. The crew had only known each other for two or three weeks – in some cases even less – but the groundwork of their relationships had been laid for the rest of the production. For now, however, it was just a relief that they were going to be able to get back to the controlled, predictable and safe environment of Pinewood Studios.

KITCHEN

Onaha, Kyrano's wife, is responsible for the majority of the cooking, although all the Tracy boys are accustomed to preparing late night snacks from time to time.

COMMAND CENTRE/ JEFF TRACY'S OFFICE

Doubling as International Rescue's Command Centre and Jeff Tracy's office, this section of Tracy Island is the nerve centre of the whole organisation. Open and spacious – like everywhere else on the island – Jeff's office provides him with plenty of opportunity to monitor rescue operations together with his many business interests.

When disaster looms, the office can be transformed into the Command Centre at the press of Jeff's hand. The mural of Jeff and his family turns into images of the Tracys, kitted out in uniform.

SATELLITE HILL

Desperate to return control to Thunderbird 5 following The Hood's takeover of the island, Alan, Fermat and Tin-Tin travel through Tracy Island's jungles to Satellite Hill. It is there that the main communicator relay to International Rescue's space station is located. The relay resembles a large steel palm tree.

THUNDERBIRD 2 LAUNCH PAD

Thunderbird 2's launch pad is cleverly disguised. Even the palm trees, which fold down when Thunderbird 2 prepares to lift off, disguise what this area of the island is actually used for.

THE LIBRARY

Like a crucible standing at the summit of the island, the library disguises the launch point for Thunderbird 3. As soon as the countdown begins, the library separates in three, the sections splitting apart to provide room for the huge rocket to lift into space.

DIVING POOL

When Thunderbird 1 takes off, the base of the pool rises up, causing water to spill out over the sides. As this happens, the larger pool, below, slides underneath, exposing the silo for International Rescue's reconnaissance ship.

MAIN SWIMMING POOL

When Thunderbird 1 is preparing to take off, the main swimming pool slides underneath the diving pool and the house itself. The Thunderbird 1 silo is located further away from the house for good reason: the heat from the rocket-plane's exhaust would cause damage to the rest of the complex.

In the two weeks of rehearsals that took place before the trip to the Seychelles, the cast had spent several long sessions reading through the script. Along with the director and writer they had discussed their characters, and their intentions, and tweaked their dialogue.

For Dominic Colenso and Lex Shrapnel, the two Tracy brothers who weren't American, these meetings also gave them the chance to test and hone their accents.

For Ron Cook, those two weeks gave him the chance to decide how he was going to portray Parker, who had been the most caricatured of all the original *Thunderbirds* puppets. Cook was keen to bring Parker to life as a full, three dimensional character.

Although Cook didn't want to distance himself too far from the original, he also didn't want to just copy it. In particular, he was concerned that the original Parker was conceived at a time when the British class divide was far more pronounced. He felt that if he didn't take this into account in his version of the chauffeur-cum-butler, the character may appear anachronistic.

The cockney accent had to stay, but Cook felt that Parker's snobbery – characterised by his inappropriate dropping or inclusion of the letter 'h' – wouldn't work for a modern audience. Taking Lady Penelope to the 'h'airport', and asking to borrow her ''airpin', were jokes from times past.

DIALOGUE TWEAKS

Perhaps the most subtle of the amendments to the dialogue related to Parker's favourite football team. While flying Alan and Fermat to Tracy Island, Lady Penelope remarks that England has won a football match. Parker lifts his hands off the steering wheel to cheer and the car careers off to one side.

In earlier drafts of the script, the team Lady P mentioned was Liverpool. During discussions about the script, Cook brought this to Jonathan Frakes' attention. Parker being a cockney, he would obviously support a London side, but which one? If he had been in prison at Parkmoor Scrubs he might have watched Tottenham Hotspur from his cell window… but then if a specific London side was chosen the film would end up alienating part of the British audience. In the end they decided to play it safe and go with England.

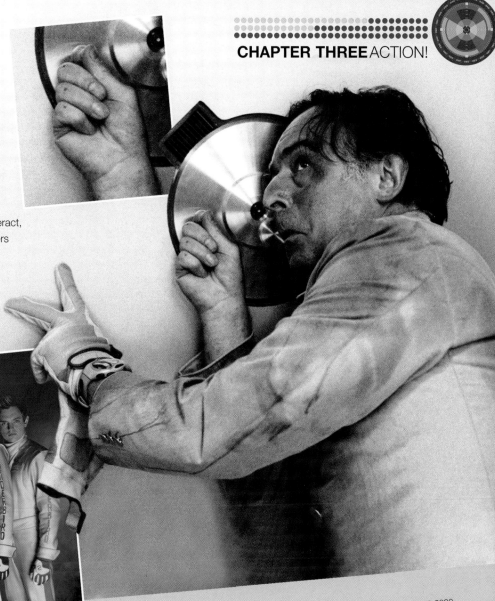

In addition, Cook was keen to acknowledge the fact that Parker had once been in prison. For this reason, small black dots – prison tattoos – were drawn on Cook's knuckles when he was being made-up, while Cook envisaged that Parker would have similar prison tattoos on his arms.

While Sophia Myles and Ron Cook were trying to work out how their characters would interact, the Tracy brothers were developing their characters in a far more physical way.

Within minutes of meeting up for the first time, a strong camaraderie developed. They began exchanging phone numbers and socialising, but also exchanging notes on their punishing physical schedule.

FINANCIAL TIMES JULY 30 2020

WEEKEND

STYLE

Pink... the new black?

London's smart set have turned pink. Who has inspired this trend? **Cordelia Posey** investigates.

Ron Cook was not the only person to have input into the script. As he and Sophia Myles began working through their dialogue, they came across a scene in which Lady Penelope was reading the *Financial Times* while Parker flew FAB 1 to Tracy Island. As the scene progressed, Frakes asked Sophia if she could ad lib some headlines from the newspaper. Quick as a flash she 'read' something from the fashion pages: 'Look here Parker, it says that pink is the new black.'

Although Ben Torgersen was in very good physical shape, having wrestled at school, there was a requirement for the other brothers to get into a similar condition. They were each assigned their own physical trainer, and three times a week they were taken through a rigorous work-out.

In addition to this work, the boys also needed to look like they spent their days in a south seas paradise. For Torgersen, Colenso and Winchester, the tanning salon beckoned, while Shrapnel went off to Spain for a fortnight to stay with his grandmother.

Perhaps it is not surprising that this aspect of their training was not altogether popular. By the end of the shoot Philip commented that next time, he would insist on fake tan!

While Dominic Colenso and Lex Shrapnel were having help from a dialogue coach, Sophia Myles had also asked if she could get some coaching. Considering herself to be 'a bit of a tom boy', Myles was concerned that she wouldn't be able to carry off Lady Penelope's style and grace. Although her voice is already quite refined, Myles spent some time with a voice coach to heighten her accent further and make sure she sounded like a right bit of posh.

Myles also had some help from a movement coach. Not accustomed to walking in high heels, she was worried that she might appear awkward. The coach concentrated on how Myles should carry herself and how she could capture the grace and elegance that the role required. When it came to performing in front of a camera, this additional training increased Myles' confidence significantly.

The need to get the group working well as a family was a major concern for Paxton and Frakes as well. They had discussed this before the start of filming, but Paxton still had doubts, especially given that he was only arriving in London the day before the start of the Pinewood shoot.

Determined to hit the ground running, he called up his five sons and arranged to meet up with them all that evening. Dominic recalls that he was going to a restaurant with his girlfriend when he got the call: 'Virgil,' a voice said, 'this is your father.'

The events of that evening have become one of the myths of the production. Meeting up together, the six began walking down London's Oxford Street, six abreast. They spotted a man on his stag night, dressed in a *Thunderbirds* costume, so they raced across the street and had a photograph taken with him.

Later, Paxton invited everyone back to his hotel suite. In the lift, regarding an older couple looking at them, Paxton introduced his companions as his sons. 'Yes,' the woman replied, 'I can see the resemblance.'

BEING JEFF TRACY

The time he spent with his five cinematic sons was as important to Bill Paxton as it was to the actors playing the Tracy brothers. Looking back on the day he met them for the first time, Paxton remembers it with fondness. 'For a moment I pretended that these were my five sons – I'm in London, I'm Jeff Tracy, and this is my family. It was a very empowering feeling. I felt invincible, I felt so virile, and it was wonderful.'

Arriving at a Chinese restaurant with the five of them he again introduced them as his children, visiting London for the first time. They were immediately obliged to take on roles, and these games helped Paxton to understand Jeff Tracy a little better. 'The idea of having five sons walking around who are all smart and sensible, it was just a great feeling. It really gave me the part; I felt I knew Jeff Tracy.'

SIR BEN KINGSLEY

Born Krishna Bhanji in Scarborough, Yorkshire, Sir Ben Kingsley changed his name early on in his career. He adopted his first name from his father, whom people called Ben, and his surname from his grandfather – a spice trader in Zanzibar who had been known as the 'Clove King'.

Although fêted by John Lennon and Ringo Starr early on in his career (Lennon told Kingsley he should go into music) he chose to ignore their advice. In 1966 he joined the Royal Shakespeare Company, alongside Patrick Stewart, and never looked back.

In 1982 Kingsley became a household name. Richard Attenborough's *Gandhi* was only Kingsley's second move, but it won him an Oscar™ for best actor and he has since been nominated three more times, most recently for *The House of Sand and Fog*.

Although he is best remembered for such heavyweight dramas as *Schindler's List* (1993) and *Death and the Maiden* (1994), Kingsley enjoys balancing these with lighter fare. In *Dave* (1993) he played the shy but principled vice-president of the United States and in *Species* (1995) he was the unscrupulous scientist Xavier Fitch.

Talking about *Thunderbirds* Kingsley says, 'I play a pantomime villain. I chew the furniture, I wear a red cape, and it's very releasing.'

THE HOOD
(TRANGH BELAGANT)

Trangh Belagant was left for dead following a disaster at his illegal diamond mine in Malaya. Jeff Tracy and International Rescue were reluctantly forced to sacrifice him, and others, in order to rescue the majority of the miners.

By sheer willpower, Belagant managed to drag his injured body out of the mine. During his slow recovery, he dwelt for many long months on the events that had taken place. The increasingly embittered Belagant determined to exact revenge on both International Rescue and the world as a whole. As his convalescence continued, Belagant began to realise that he possessed remarkable mental powers: he was able to move objects and control the minds of others. As he recovered his physical strength, Belagant – or The Hood, as he had now renamed himself – began to hone these extraordinary powers.

At the same time The Hood began accumulating the resources he would need to achieve his diabolical ends. Like Jeff Tracy before him, he began searching for individuals who could provide additional support. It was this search that led him to the brilliant Transom and the thuggish Mullion.

The Hood is committed to achieving his ends with the least effort possible. While Mullion would have attacked Tracy Island head on, The Hood is quite happy to create a distraction on Thunderbird 5. Unable to feel sympathy for others, The Hood does not care who he hurts along the way. The damage wreaked on the London Monorail could have been avoided, but The Hood is too evil to care.

ROSE KEEGAN

Following a small role in *First Knight* (1995), *Thunderbirds* is Rose Keegan's second feature film. As a child, Keegan was a fan of Fred Astaire and Ginger Rogers movies; she says she was subsequently drawn to acting because she loved being something she wasn't.

A people-watcher by dint of habit, Keegan loves studying individuals and then creating characters by combining various traits. Although a large proportion of her acting work has been in the theatre, Keegan is probably best known for the role of Sinead Creagh in the television series *Hearts and Bones*.

TRANSOM

Just as Jeff Tracy needed Brains' brilliant mind in order to build the Thunderbirds, so The Hood need someone to realise his own nefarious designs. This person was Transom.

When The Hood offered her a position in his operation, Transom leapt at the chance. These opportunities and Transom's own sympathy for The Hood came to cloud her judgement. It was only as the death of innocent people became a definite possibility that she began to realise exactly what she had signed up for.

DEOBIA OPAREI

Unusually for young, contemporary actors, Deobia did not go to drama school. After participating in the National Youth Theatre, he joined a Scottish touring company before moving on to the RSC and the Royal National Theatre.

Deobia is probably best known for his role as Le Chocolat in *Moulin Rouge!* (2001), although he can also be spotted in *Alien[3]* (1992).

After completing work on *Thunderbirds*, Deobia moved to Australia.

MULLION

Although not particularly bright, Mullion is physically very dangerous and a menace to Alan and his friends as they race to rescue Jeff Tracy. Fortunately for them, Mullion's size and strength occasionally result in clumsiness and the children are more than capable of outsmarting him.

Unlike Transom, the mercenary Mullion has no feelings of loyalty to The Hood. As soon as they have finished robbing the banks of the world, Mullion has every intention of moving on.

THE HOOD'S SUBMARINE

The Hood's technological resources may not quite match the vehicles at the disposal of International Rescue, but he does possess a remarkable submarine which is capable of incredible speeds. Within a day of the oil rig disaster The Hood has tracked the Thunderbirds to Tracy Island and is ready to bring about their downfall.

Of course, speed isn't the only impressive feature of The Hood's underwater transport. This stealthy vehicle is capable of amazing speeds and is able to remain almost entirely undetected beneath the ocean waves. The vessel can pass through clear waters or beneath the bow of a military submarine and yet seem totally invisible.

Designed and developed by The Hood's accomplice Transom, the submersible is not restricted to deep water ports. As it approached Tracy Island it was actually able to mount the beach, enabling the crew to walk straight onto dry land. It is also equipped with sophisticated tracing facilities. By monitoring communications between Tracy Island and Thunderbird 5, Transom was able to pinpoint the exact location of International Rescue's space station. With the location confirmed, a sea-to-space missile was fired and The Hood's nefarious scheme progressed to its next stage.

THE SCALE OF THUNDERBIRDS

For many of the actors taking part in *Thunderbirds* this was their first major motion picture. Arriving on the Pinewood stages for the first time, they were astonished by what they saw.

Rose Keegan, the actress playing Transom, had spent her early years living on military bases where her father was working. For her, the size and complexity of the sets, and the huge number of people involved in the shoot, seemed almost military in its efficiency and planning.

To Brady Corbet, there was no comparison between *Thunderbirds* and his previous film, the art house movie *Thirteen*. The budget for that film had been so low that the dolly took the form of a shopping trolley, and when the car used in the production broke it had to be pushed along by the crew.

What was most astonishing to the actors was just how much had actually been built, and the level of detail that had been achieved. The cockpits of the craft were all intact, and when the actors pushed buttons lights would actually illuminate. In the Tracys' house a full swimming pool had been put in place, there was a stream running through one of the rooms, and even the elevators worked.

Arriving on the set at the start of rehearsals, the four Tracy brothers were greeted by Jonathan Frakes and taken down to the stage to be shown around. Standing back and opening his arms wide, Frakes said, 'Go play.'

OIL RIG RESCUE

The oil rig rescue was the most complex sequence to capture in almost every respect. Although much of it was going to be completed using CGI, a large proportion of this sequence – the section featuring Virgil on the Rescue Platform – was going to be shot for real.

In order to accomplish this, a large section of the oil rig had been built to full scale. As Dominic Colenso hung onto the Rescue Platform, that was itself swinging about in mid-air, rain was being hurled at him, the 'sea' in the tank below was surging and falling, and stunt men were throwing themselves off the rig and into the water.

At the same time, Dominic was trying to extinguish flames and pull the oil rig workers to safety.

DOMINIC COLENSO

One of two British actors playing Tracy brothers, Colenso had only recently finished training at Drama Centre when he was offered the role of Virgil. Daunted by the requirement to have an American accent, Colenso was concerned this would prevent him from getting the role. Indeed, following the first audition, casting director Mary Selway had told him to go away and work on it a little more.

Jonathan Frakes' enthusiasm at the second interview left Colenso feeling hopeful about getting the part, but in the three months between auditioning and hearing how he had done, Colenso had almost forgotten about the whole thing.

Brought up in Oxfordshire, Colenso moved with his family to Düsseldorf, Germany, when he was 16 years old. Following the move he began travelling widely, even teaching for a time in Africa. This experience has led him to begin sponsoring Tanzanian students.

Following the completion of *Thunderbirds*, Colenso has appered in episodes of the television dramas *Doctors* and *Midsomer Murders*.

VIRGIL TRACY

More reflective and thoughtful than his exuberant and cocky elder brother, Scott, Virgil is regarded as a safe pair of hands by his father.

Co-pilot of Thunderbird 2, a powerful ship which he flies with his father, Virgil needs every ounce of concentration to pilot it effectively. This was particularly the case in the foul weather conditions that existed during the oil rig rescue.

As well as requiring focussed pilots, Thunderbird 2 also needs its crew to be versatile. The ship is designed to transport a vast array of vehicles all over the globe – the Mole, the Thunderizer, the Firefly – and Virgil has to turn his hand to all of them.

RESCUE PLATFORM

Sometimes the only way to reach survivors is in the air. Because of its size and the downdrafts it causes, Thunderbird 2 is generally unable to get close to unstable buildings. It is at these times that the Rescue Platform is lowered from a central section of Thunderbird 2's pod. Lowered on a cable, the platform can be positioned next to the windows of tall buildings, allowing survivors to clamber out and into safety.

In the case of the oil rig rescue, the high winds and driving rain meant that the platform could not be dropped very far. Instead, a series of rescue lines were fired to the oil rig workers. Shot from a special gun, these lines were rocket propelled and laser guided. Once the workers had grabbed a line, they attached themselves to it and were hauled up to the Rescue Platform.

As soon as they reached safety, the platform was raised up into the pod, allowing Virgil to undertake emergency first aid while Thunderbird 2 raced to an emergency medical facility in San Francisco.

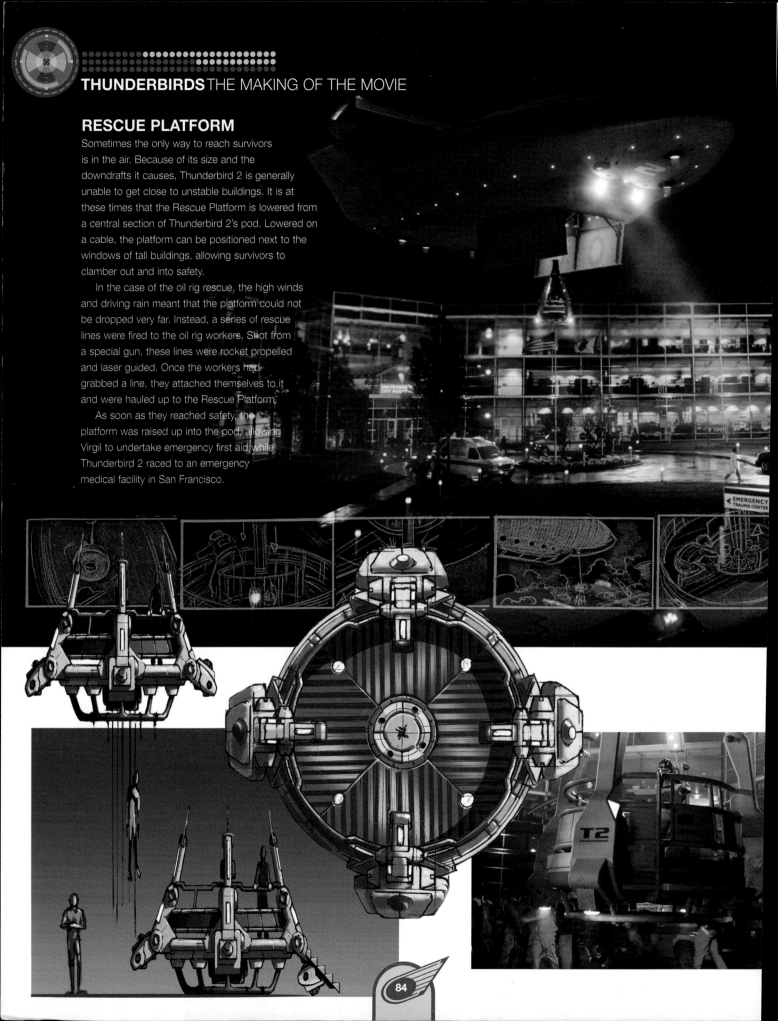

BEHIND THE LENS

Jonathan Frakes has enjoyed a reputation as an actor's director since his early days directing episodes of *Star Trek: The Next Generation*. The episode *Offspring*, in which the android Data creates his own child, is considered a favourite by many of the series' actors.

Having been an actor himself, Frakes had experienced frustration with directors so involved with the technical aspects of their role that they only provided limited guidance to their cast. From his first time behind the camera, Frakes had determined not to make the same mistake. Each person is different and he had learned to respect that, developing a range of techniques that could be used to bring out their best possible performance.

Directing children required these techniques to be brought into even sharper focus. During the two weeks of rehearsals on *Thunderbirds*, Frakes got to know the young stars. 'Brady's knowledge of films and filmmaking is encyclopaedic,' he says. 'Soren's energy and intelligence and instincts are far beyond his age and Vanessa is an absolute delight. What's more, all three of them are not just physically attractive but you can feel how clever they are.'

Confident in their abilities, Frakes now saw his job as 'wrangling all their energy into the same focus, to get all of them in the same frame of mind at the same time when doing a scene.' Whereas experienced actors know how to conserve and maintain their energy levels ('they know how many coffees to drink in the morning, they know how much to eat and when') these younger actors didn't have that experience. Therefore, Frakes saw it as his job to guide, steer and control their energy. 'It's like herding cats,' he says, laughing.

With all the cast, if Frakes wanted to give someone a pointer he would go over and talk to them personally. He had worked with directors who shouted instructions across the set and he felt that this tended to reduce trust. Instead, with less experienced actors he would even whisper ideas into their ear, just before shouting 'action'.

Frakes' legendary energy and enthusiasm would also, at times, get the better of him. Following one take involving Lex Shrapnel, Frakes turned to him and joked, 'Lex, that was… that was William Shatner.'

With actors like Sir Ben Kingsley and Ron Cook, Frakes would leave them to play a little more. After watching Kingsley perform a scene, Phil Winchester noted that he would do a take and then, 'by amending his inflection or changing the punctuation he would alter the whole meaning of a line.'

Ron Cook's performance reminded Frakes of Brent Spiner, the actor who plays Data in *Star Trek*. Just as they were wrapping up a scene, Cook would often turn to Frakes saying, 'Just give me one more, I've got an idea.'

'I'd always just let him have it,' says Frakes, 'because 80 per cent of the time it was something great and I just looked like a hero.'

PROFILE BRENDAN GALVIN – DIRECTOR OF PHOTOGRAPHY

Dublin-born Brendan Galvin has worked on such films as *The Commitments* (1991) and *Far and* Away (1992), but it is with more recent movies like *Behind Enemy Lines* (2001) and *Veronica Guerin* (2003) that he has made his name as a director of photography.

Galvin's role on *Thunderbirds* involved helping Frakes capture the energy he was trying to create with the actors. Galvin was responsible for the lighting and suggesting the right mix of shots to realise the director's vision. He is currently working on a remake of the 1965 film *The Flight of the Phoenix*.

A HAPPY SET

As the pace of production began to increase, one of the big challenges for Frakes was to keep the cast and crew relaxed and happy.

Each morning, fiirst assistant director Tommy Gormley would lead the crew in singing 'Happy Birthday' to anyone who was celebrating that day. If it wasn't anyone's birthday they would sing it anyway.

On one occasion, when tensions began to rise on the stage and the atmosphere became fraught, Frakes took matters into his own hands. Doing a passable impression of a histrionic director, Frakes succeeded in raising a laugh.

All of these techniques accord with Frakes' particular philosophy about directing. 'I always feel that if I can create an atmosphere in which people can make mistakes without being afraid of making mistakes, without being afraid of being reprimanded, or hurt or made to feel guilty, then people will play… and if people are free to play then sometimes magic will happen.'

As the shoot progressed, those actors not required for the current scene would busy themselves trying to make time pass.

When they weren't maintaining their skin tone in the tanning salon, the Tracy brothers spent their time stealing the golf carts used by the runners and racing around Pinewood.

For Ron Cook, Sophia Myles, Rose Keegan and Deobia Oparei, much of their time was spent training for a fight sequence that was to take place during the second act of the movie. For two weeks they trained for five hours a day, choreographing the fight sequence and getting into shape so that the filming of the scene would be as swift and efficient as possible.

PENELOPE TO THE RESCUE

'The Thunderbirds appear to be in a spot of trouble. And I don't like that.' With those words, Lady Penelope and Parker get inside FAB 1 and take to the air, heading in the direction of Tracy Island.

Only minutes earlier, Lady Penelope had been reclining in her capacious bath tub, surrounded by bubbles and sipping a cup of freshly brewed tea. Penelope had discovered that the oil rig disaster of the day before had been the result of an act of sabotage. What's more, one of the workers rescued by Thunderbird 2 was in fact an impostor. As she explained, this individual – a man called Mullion – worked with a woman called Transom. Together, they were employees of The Hood.

Parker immediately recognised that The Hood must be an alias. Penelope had already reached that conclusion and learned that he was in fact Trangh Belagant, the one time owner of an illegal diamond mine. When the mine collapsed some ten years earlier he had been presumed killed. Obviously, this assumption was wrong.

What made Lady Penelope's investigations more pressing was the fact that The Hood's brother was Jeff Tracy's manservant, Kyrano. Also, the Thunderbirds had failed to respond to a series of international emergencies: a typhoon was striking Singapore, a bridge in Buenos Aires had collapsed, and Jakarta was suffering a volcanic eruption.

Climbing delicately out of her bath, Lady Penelope crossed the floor to her vast walk-in wardrobe and began discussing her hectic social schedule with Parker. She was supposed to be clay pigeon shooting and attending a benefit gala for the Institute for the Blind. To avoid these engagements she would feign a broken shooting arm and buy a dozen guide dogs.

Now, as they hurtled through the skies to a small, secret island in the depths of the Pacific, Parker and Penelope were ready for action. The Thunderbirds might have been in trouble, but soon all that was going to change.

Lady Penelope finally steps out- dressed in a stunning ensemble, hair impossibly dry and make-up perfect.

LADY PENELOPE
The Thunderbirds appear to be in a spot of trouble. And I don't like that.

INT/EXT. FAB 1 - CREIGHTON WARD MANSION DRIVEWAY - DAY   105

As FAB 1 hurtles down the driveway, the back bumper folds down and huge JET NOZZLES SLIDE OUT. WINGS EXTEND on both sides and the grill reconfigures into an aerodynamic shape. Then FAB 1 STREAKS UP INTO THE SKY, the wheels retracting.

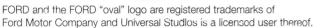

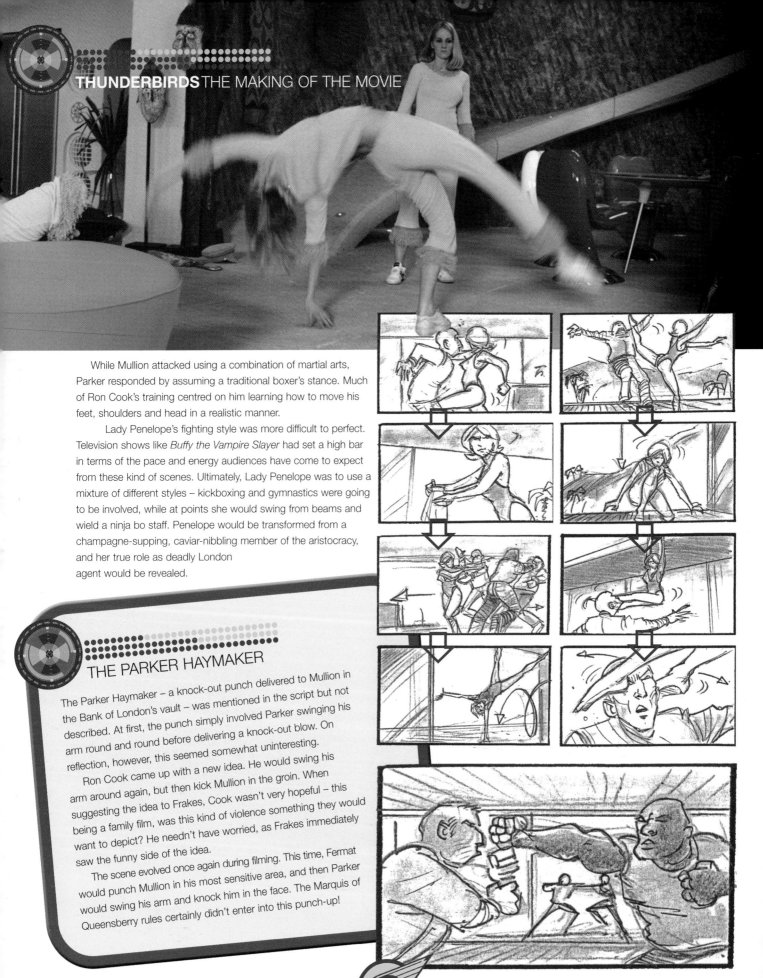

While Mullion attacked using a combination of martial arts, Parker responded by assuming a traditional boxer's stance. Much of Ron Cook's training centred on him learning how to move his feet, shoulders and head in a realistic manner.

Lady Penelope's fighting style was more difficult to perfect. Television shows like *Buffy the Vampire Slayer* had set a high bar in terms of the pace and energy audiences have come to expect from these kind of scenes. Ultimately, Lady Penelope was to use a mixture of different styles – kickboxing and gymnastics were going to be involved, while at points she would swing from beams and wield a ninja bo staff. Penelope would be transformed from a champagne-supping, caviar-nibbling member of the aristocracy, and her true role as deadly London agent would be revealed.

THE PARKER HAYMAKER

The Parker Haymaker – a knock-out punch delivered to Mullion in the Bank of London's vault – was mentioned in the script but not described. At first, the punch simply involved Parker swinging his arm round and round before delivering a knock-out blow. On reflection, however, this seemed somewhat uninteresting.

Ron Cook came up with a new idea. He would swing his arm around again, but then kick Mullion in the groin. When suggesting the idea to Frakes, Cook wasn't very hopeful – this being a family film, was this kind of violence something they would want to depict? He needn't have worried, as Frakes immediately saw the funny side of the idea.

The scene evolved once again during filming. This time, Fermat would punch Mullion in his most sensitive area, and then Parker would swing his arm and knock him in the face. The Marquis of Queensberry rules certainly didn't enter into this punch-up!

SOREN FULTON

Soren Fulton learned three important things while filming *Thunderbirds*: that the Seychelles is not the best working environment; to never apply sun tan oil when you have sand on your hands; and to be careful which trees to rest your hands on – some Seychelles trees have barbs!

Fulton also discovered that you should be careful what you ask for. After yearning to return to the milder climate of the UK, Fulton discovered that England could produce its own extremes of temperature. It was a very bitter day when Fulton did the location filming for the scenes set outside Alan and Fermat's school. In between takes, both he and Brady Corbet spent their time wrapped in blankets and sipping hot drinks.

The youngest member of the *Thunderbirds* cast, Fulton has appeared in a range of television series, including *Frasier* and *Charmed*, while his film credits include *Face to Face* (2001) and *Ring of Endless Light* (2002).

FERMAT

Alan's loyal school-friend and companion, Fermat is to the youngest of the Tracys what Brains is to Jeff. Fermat's keen intelligence and mental agility complements Alan's physical prowess. Wise beyond his years, Fermat's maturity has also helped to keep Alan's wilder imaginings in check.

Although two years younger than Alan, Fermat's brilliance has been apparent from a very young age. Remarkably, Fermat is the only person on Tracy Island who can talk on the same level as Brains. Fermat clearly enjoys visiting his father's laboratory and learning from him.

This learning is not always one way though. Fermat's skill with a computer is second to none and, following The Hood's invasion of the island, it is ultimately down to him to restore control to Thunderbird 5.

This isn't the only way in which Fermat proves himself. Although he usually relies on his brain to get him through situations, during the monorail rescue Fermat is left to pilot Thunderbird 2 on his own.

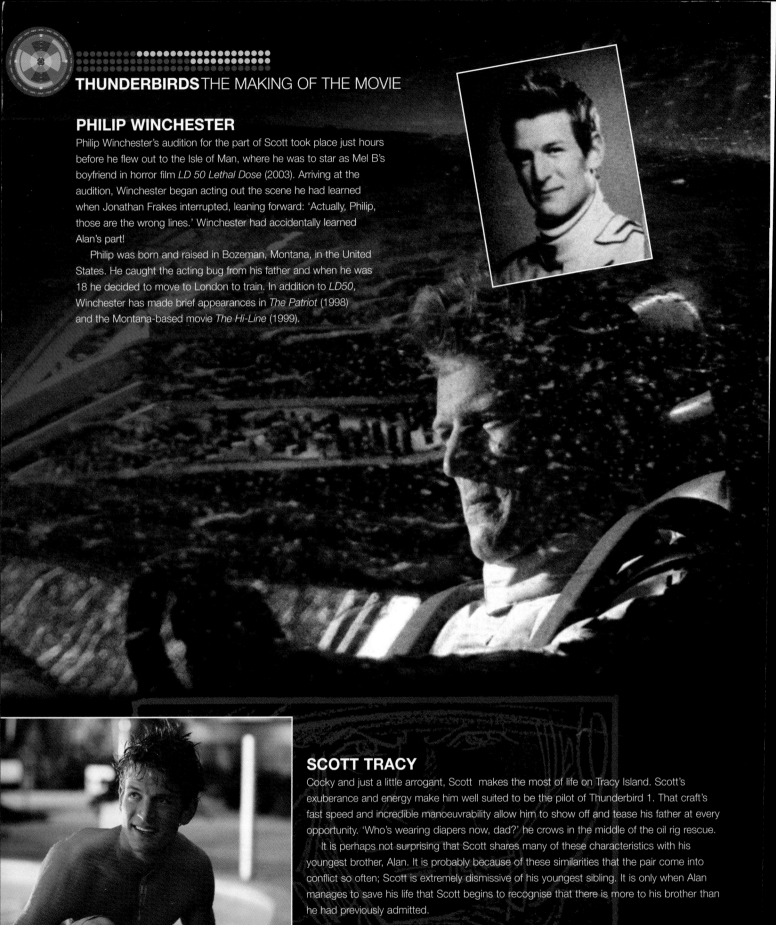

PHILIP WINCHESTER

Philip Winchester's audition for the part of Scott took place just hours before he flew out to the Isle of Man, where he was to star as Mel B's boyfriend in horror film *LD 50 Lethal Dose* (2003). Arriving at the audition, Winchester began acting out the scene he had learned when Jonathan Frakes interrupted, leaning forward: 'Actually, Philip, those are the wrong lines.' Winchester had accidentally learned Alan's part!

Philip was born and raised in Bozeman, Montana, in the United States. He caught the acting bug from his father and when he was 18 he decided to move to London to train. In addition to *LD50*, Winchester has made brief appearances in *The Patriot* (1998) and the Montana-based movie *The Hi-Line* (1999).

SCOTT TRACY

Cocky and just a little arrogant, Scott makes the most of life on Tracy Island. Scott's exuberance and energy make him well suited to be the pilot of Thunderbird 1. That craft's fast speed and incredible manoeuvrability allow him to show off and tease his father at every opportunity. 'Who's wearing diapers now, dad?' he crows in the middle of the oil rig rescue.

It is perhaps not surprising that Scott shares many of these characteristics with his youngest brother, Alan. It is probably because of these similarities that the pair come into conflict so often; Scott is extremely dismissive of his youngest sibling. It is only when Alan manages to save his life that Scott begins to recognise that there is more to his brother than he had previously admitted.

THUNDERBIRD 1 – THE SHIP OF DOOM

The sequences that turned out to be most challenging for many of the actors were those shot in the Thunderbird 1 cockpit. The movement of the characters as Thunderbird 1 flew to London was not going to be captured by simply wobbling the camera. The cockpit was placed on a gimbal that would move from side-to-side, shaking the actors as required.

If this wasn't enough to make the cast feel slightly nauseous, the set was also small and claustrophobic, and the seats extremely uncomfortable. The actors were strapped in and various parts of the set were locked into place around them. If any of the cast felt the urge to go to the toilet they would have to wait for a break in production!

During a particularly arduous two days strapped inside Thunderbird 1, a number of the cast started to suffer from motion sickness. Indeed, Brady Corbet found the whole experience so exhausting that, during a close-up of Sophia Myles, he fell asleep at the controls.

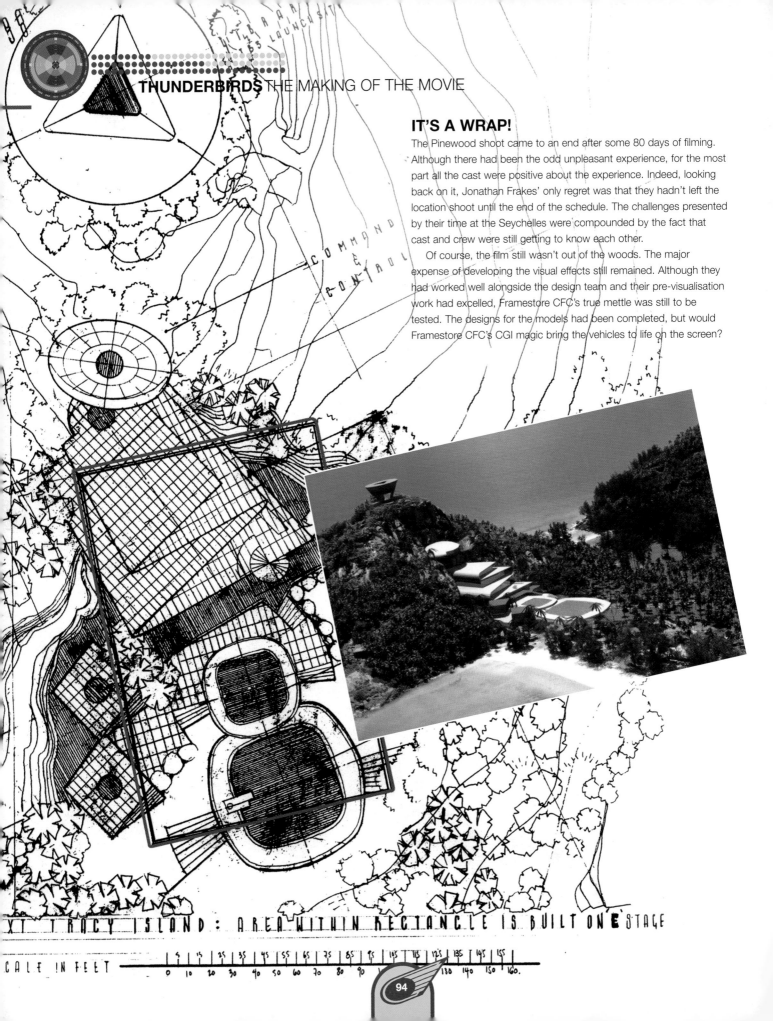

IT'S A WRAP!

The Pinewood shoot came to an end after some 80 days of filming. Although there had been the odd unpleasant experience, for the most part all the cast were positive about the experience. Indeed, looking back on it, Jonathan Frakes' only regret was that they hadn't left the location shoot until the end of the schedule. The challenges presented by their time at the Seychelles were compounded by the fact that cast and crew were still getting to know each other.

Of course, the film still wasn't out of the woods. The major expense of developing the visual effects still remained. Although they had worked well alongside the design team and their pre-visualisation work had excelled, Framestore CFC's true mettle was still to be tested. The designs for the models had been completed, but would Framestore CFC's CGI magic bring the vehicles to life on the screen?

XT TRACY ISLAND : AREA WITHIN RECTANGLE IS BUILT ON E STAGE

CALE IN FEET

CHAPTER FOUR
LIFT-OFF

SOME directors make no distinction between production and post-production – for them the entire filmmaking process is all production. This would certainly be true of *Thunderbirds*. With Framestore CFC involved almost from the very start of the movie's development, collaborating on the designs and undertaking the pre-visualisation, distinctions like pre- and post-production seemed almost arbitrary.

When the focus shifted to filming the live action sequences, Framestore CFC continued with the development of the CGI. Computer models had been built of the craft and vehicles and now it was time to begin animating them, to get them moving and flying.

It was only at this point that Framestore CFC began to realise just how demanding this film was going to be. Most effects-heavy movies belong to a specific genre: they are space operas, like *Star Trek*, *Star Wars*, or even *Galaxy Quest*; they take place underwater, as is the case with *U-571* or *K19: The Widowmaker*; or they may feature sequences set in the air, such as *Pearl Harbor*.

In each of these films the effects sequences are generally very specific, thus allowing the CGI developers to specialise and focus

their energies. With *Thunderbirds* there was no such luxury. 'What makes this film special is that you've got several genres in one,' comments visual effects supervisor Mike McGee. 'In this film we have aerial effects, space and underwater sequences, and all of these have to marry up.'

This wasn't the only pressure Framestore CFC was under. The launch sequences for Thunderbirds 1, 2 and 3 all required vast, billowing clouds of smoke. Although a handful of films had included CGI smoke effects in the past, these effects had been relatively subtle and inconspicuous. In *Thunderbirds*, this smoke would be much more prominent.

One of the reasons Jonathan Frakes was chosen to direct *Thunderbirds* was his experience with visual effects. In particular, he had developed a reputation for delivering films where the effects look like they cost more than they actually did.

Frakes was relatively unphased by the challenges ahead: 'I don't know how the effects people do it, but I know when it's good. As a great cartoonist once said, "I don't know much about it, but I know what I like."'

THUNDERBIRD 4

The hazards faced by mankind can occur underwater, just as much as on land or in space. It is for this reason that International Rescue chose to develop their own submersible rescue craft – Thunderbird 4.

Small and highly manoeuvrable, the strength of this diminutive submarine seems disproportionately great – it is able to lift and carry burdens many times its own weight. This ability is the product of good design. When he first began work on Thunderbird 4, Brains realised the craft would sometimes need to fit into very small spaces. Although it might not look like much, Thunderbird 4 is actually able to travel to depths of ten miles – three miles beyond the deepest ocean. The craft's robotic arms are designed to be versatile: they can clamp onto vessels that have lost power, clear a rock fall, or even pick up an injured body. Nothing is too much for this yellow submarine!

Although Thunderbird 4 has its own exit from Tracy Island's underground silos, generally speaking it is ferried to disaster situations aboard Thunderbird 2. In order to exit its pod, Thunderbird 2 hovers over a body of water, partially lowers the pod and allows Thunderbird 4 to simply slide into the waters below.

Although it can be piloted by one individual, Thunderbird 4 ideally has two pilots. Only then can the robotic arms be controlled with sufficient delicacy. While underwater, entry to the submersible can be gained from a rear airlock. During the monorail rescue this is how Tin-Tin manages to get on board the ship after attaching the cable to the monorail carriage.

FINS

Thunderbird 4's ventral and side fins are vital both in providing the craft with stability and in helping it to steer effectively.

ENGINES

The two cylindrical engines suck in and dispel water with astonishing force. The underwater equivalent of a jet engine, this allows the craft to race through the oceans at incredible speeds.

AIRLOCK

When Thunderbird 4 is too large or too cumbersome to effect a rescue on its own, its crew is able to proceed in diving gear, exiting the craft through the rear airlock. The airlock is designed to cycle air out and water in at very high speeds, in the knowledge that, during a rescue, time is very often at a premium.

ROBOTIC ARMS

Flexible and extendible, Thunderbird 4's robotic arms are suitable for a range of scenarios. When not in use they simply fold up and are tucked underneath the cockpit.

SPECIFICATIONS

LENGTH: 30 feet
WIDTH: 11 feet
SURFACE CRUISING SPEED: 40 knots
UNDERWATER SPEED: 160 knots
RECOMMENDED CREW: 2

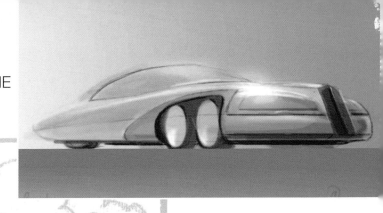

DESIGNING FAB 1

In many ways FAB 1 was the biggest challenge faced by the combined teams of John Beard's designers and Framestore CFC. It is not just one of the most famous, popular and iconic vehicles of the original series, it was also the only one that would actually have to be built for real. Unlike all the Thunderbird craft, FAB 1 would have to be driven, and this presented unique hurdles that needed to be overcome.

In many ways, the challenge of realising FAB 1 was actually a metaphor for the film as a whole. Just as the movie was a heady mix of different genres – space, underwater and aerial adventure – so FAB 1 was a futuristic, modern day Chitty Chitty Bang Bang. It was a normal car, but also travelled on water like the original FAB 1 and could fly through the air. What's more, somewhere along the way, Parker and Lady Penelope were going to have to abandon ship and take to the waves on a pink pedalo.

Making all of this believable, and squeezing all these elements into FAB 1's 28 feet, was never going to be easy. Just about everyone in Beard's team had a stab at the concept art for FAB 1 and countless variations resulted. Just about the only thing they had in common were six wheels and the colour pink.

In some of the initial designs for the car, it was very similar to the original FAB 1 – a large Rolls-Royce or limousine, with a relatively small driving cabin and a large open space for Lady Penelope to lounge in. As the demands of the story increased and the team were asked to include more and more elements, this space began to shrink.

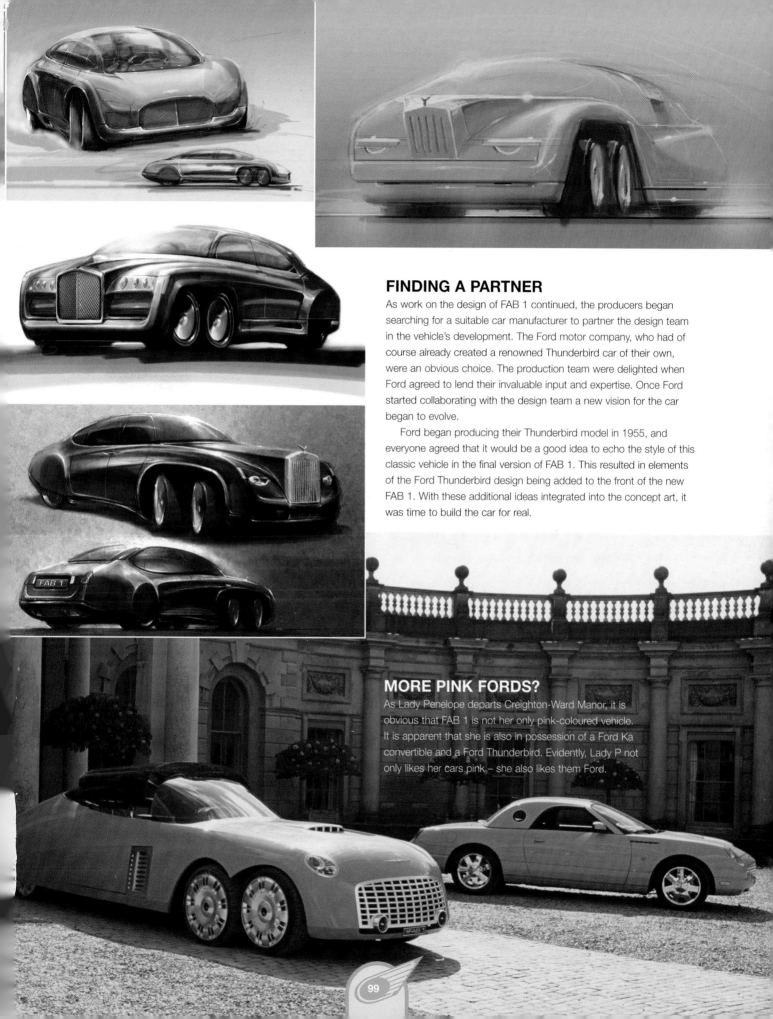

FINDING A PARTNER

As work on the design of FAB 1 continued, the producers began searching for a suitable car manufacturer to partner the design team in the vehicle's development. The Ford motor company, who had of course already created a renowned Thunderbird car of their own, were an obvious choice. The production team were delighted when Ford agreed to lend their invaluable input and expertise. Once Ford started collaborating with the design team a new vision for the car began to evolve.

Ford began producing their Thunderbird model in 1955, and everyone agreed that it would be a good idea to echo the style of this classic vehicle in the final version of FAB 1. This resulted in elements of the Ford Thunderbird design being added to the front of the new FAB 1. With these additional ideas integrated into the concept art, it was time to build the car for real.

MORE PINK FORDS?

As Lady Penelope departs Creighton-Ward Manor, it is obvious that FAB 1 is not her only pink-coloured vehicle. It is apparent that she is also in possession of a Ford Ka convertible and a Ford Thunderbird. Evidently, Lady P not only likes her cars pink – she also likes them Ford.

FAB 1 IN THE FLESH

By the time design work began on FAB 1, a close relationship had developed between the art department and Framestore CFC. While the designers would come up with an overall look and feel for a vehicle, Framestore CFC's modellers would then take these ideas and begin fleshing them out on their computers.

For Framestore CFC, FAB 1 was the biggest challenge they had faced so far. 'We knew it had to be a car and a plane and a boat,' says Mark Nelmes, 'and our CG guys got very wrapped up in the pure mechanics of it. For them it's very important that the car could actually work. All our vehicles were made in such a way that they could actually be manufactured.'

With this in mind, the car's design went back and forth several more times before Framestore CFC and the design team were ready to take it to Ford's design laboratory. Ford had begun building their own version of the car, and the designers and Framestore CFC were able to offer them additional feedback.

Looking at Ford's model they determined that its rear needed to be slightly larger in order to accommodate the jet engine. In this, and a number of other ways, the design expanded to fit what needed to be put inside.

These weren't the only challenges that Ford needed to overcome. Every car has its own turning circle, determined by its two front wheels. Since FAB 1 has two sets of front wheels it effectively has two distinct turning circles. For this reason, the two pairs of front wheels had to be able to rotate at slightly different angles.

FAB 1

It is possible to describe Lady Penelope Creighton-Ward in just three words: stylish, elegant and pink. These are certainly adjectives that can also be applied to her remarkable Ford Thunderbird.

As is the case with Lady Penelope herself, nothing about this vehicle is as it seems. FAB 1 can fly through the air and ride on water, and comes eqipped with an anti-missile defence system. The car is designed to deal with every situation that can possibly be imagined.

Driven, or rather piloted, by Parker, FAB 1 contains a luxurious passenger area. While Parker transports her between engagements, Lady P catches up on the news, talks to friends and associates, and – wherever possible – sups champagne that is stored in a chilled compartment next to her seat.

She might never lose her cool, but Lady Penelope is always prepared for every eventuality. In the event that FAB 1 is destroyed or damaged, it even has its own escape capsule in the form of a pink pedalo. Although it doesn't have a motor, Parker is able to power this vehicle himself, while his mistress reclines behind him.

At the end of term, Lady Penelope arrives at Alan and Fermat's school to return them to Tracy Island for the holidays. As they leave the building she scolds Alan for almost revealing that she is a secret agent. 'Please,' she says, as they walk towards her extraordinary car, 'I'm trying to keep a low profile.'

CANOPY

The British climate may be improving, but it is still subject to damp spells. Although she enjoys travelling open top, Lady Penelope raises no objections when Parker raises FAB 1's canopy into position – particularly when the car is about to burst into the skies or settle onto the sea.

PARKER'S VISOR

When FAB 1 converts into a plane, a piloting visor drops down from Parker's chauffeur's hat. This visor provides him with vital data regarding the vehicle's altitude, speed, location and its pitch and yaw.

HYDROFOIL

There are times when it isn't possible for FAB 1 to land on terra firma, or when Lady Penelope prefers to travel on water. It is then that FAB 1 converts into a boat or, more accurately, a hydrofoil.

SOPHIA MYLES

The casting of Lady Penelope was unique in that the prospective actresses were asked to screen-test in costume. Both Frakes and the producers knew that whoever got the role would have to carry off Lady P's strident pink wardrobe.

Never having watched *Thunderbirds* as a child, Myles initially failed to understand the significance of the role. She soon realised, however, that Lady Penelope was one of the best-loved characters in the original series.

Having little interest in fashion – 'If Gap was the only shop I'd be happy' – working with costume designer Marit Allen opened Myles' eyes, and she learned a lot about style and accessories.

Best known for her portrayal of the vampire Erika in the horror movie *Underworld* (2003), Myles has also appeared in *From Hell* (2001) and *Out of Bounds* (2003).

LADY PENELOPE CREIGHTON–WARD

She might appear to be just another member of the English aristocracy but this is just a cover. Behind the formal engagements and hectic social life, Lady Penelope Creighton-Ward pursues a secret role as International Rescue's London Agent.

Although she is just one of International Rescue's many point-men, it is to her that Jeff Tracy turns most often. Over the years the pair have become very close and he often contacts her when he wants to talk through problems in the Tracy household.

The ever-present Parker helps her to fulfil her role as one of International Rescue's most formidable allies.

RON COOK

When casting the role of Parker, Jonathan Frakes recalls seeing a 'smorgasbord of brilliant actors'. Of the 40 people that he saw, Frakes thought eight would have been 'brilliant' for the role, but Ron Cook was that much better. 'Physically, he just looks the part,' says Frakes.

'To his credit,' Frakes continues, 'all the actors who wanted the part sheepishly called the casting director to ask "who ended up getting Parker?" When they heard it was Ron Cook they remarked, "oh, oh good." There seems to be some kind of mutual admiration society among actors for Ron.'

A character actor with a vast array of theatre, television and film work behind him, Cook is able to tuck himself so tightly into his parts that he is rarely recognised on the street. Whether this continues to be the case following *Thunderbirds* is another matter.

Although he spent the early years of his career doing educational theatre, it was not long before Cook decided to begin treading the boards for real. In a career that has spanned four decades he has come to play roles as diverse as Napoleon, Lloyd George, and Isambard Kingdom Brunel. It is thought that *Thunderbirds* is his first role as a chauffeur.

'NOSEY' PARKER

Lady Penelope's trusty chauffeur and butler is proud to call himself a true cockney. Although now a skilled butler, Parker was a convicted safe-cracker before he joined Lady Penelope's service. There was nothing that he couldn't do with a bit of wire, or so it was said in criminal circles. It was inevitable that this sorry trade would eventually land him in trouble. Caught red-handed, he was found guilty and thrown into Parkmoor Scrubs for an extended stay at Her Majesty's pleasure.

Parker's subsequent meeting with Penelope was the beginning of an outstanding partnership: Parker an unequalled butler yet not afraid to use force in order to get his way and Penelope forever poised, elegant and enchanting.

ANIMATING THUNDERBIRDS

3D wireframe models of the Thunderbird vehicles had been created by Framestore CFC during pre-production. Once this work was completed, the time came to animate them.

During the main shoot various background images, or plates, had been filmed, across which the Thunderbird vehicles would be seen moving. In many ways, the process of capturing movement across such plates is rather like old-fashioned stop-motion filming. On a frame-by-frame basis, the 3D ships would be pasted onto the plates with their position being altered slightly on each frame. They would then effectively be photographed – in this instance

saved into the memory of a computer.

Once this process was completed, the CG artists had the equivalent of a negative which needed to be developed. This development process is called rendering and takes up to five or six hours per frame.

Once all the frames had been rendered the CG artist was then able to run them together, as they would a piece of film, to see how the movement of the ships actually looked. In general, this movement would then have to be tweaked and re-rendered somewhere between five and ten times.

STYLES OF MOVEMENT

Right at the beginning of Framestore CFC's involvement, Visual Effects Supervisors Mark Nelmes and Mike McGee talked with Jonathan Frakes about how the different Thunderbird craft should move. Frakes was very specific about what he was looking for.

Thunderbird 1 is International Rescue's reconnaissance vehicle, so Frakes wanted it to be small and fast, able to dart about quickly, stop, hover and tip its nose, and then race off again. For reference, Framestore CFC staff looked at footage of the American F-16 fighter.

Frakes frequently referred to Thunderbird 2 as the workhorse of the fleet. He wanted to be able to feel the sheer weight and size of this craft in the way that it flew. As they tried to capture its movement, the Framestore CFC artists imagined the ship as a huge jumbo jet and

tried to visualise the kind of downdrafts it would generate if it was hovering in the air.

Finding inspiration for Thunderbird 3 was much easier – for this they simply looked at the American Space Shuttle.

In part, the sense of movement would be emphasised by each ship' overall look. Whereas Thunderbirds 1 and 3 would look very shiny and new, Thunderbird 2 was to be a little more weather-beaten – a little more scuffed and battered.

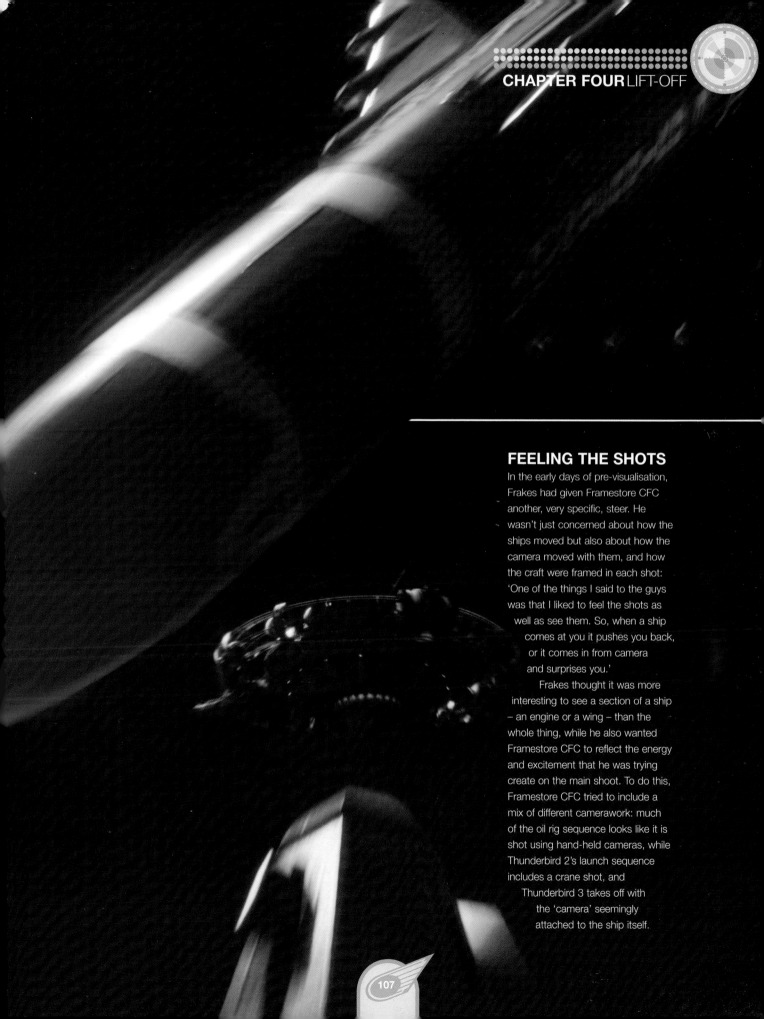

FEELING THE SHOTS

In the early days of pre-visualisation, Frakes had given Framestore CFC another, very specific, steer. He wasn't just concerned about how the ships moved but also about how the camera moved with them, and how the craft were framed in each shot: 'One of the things I said to the guys was that I liked to feel the shots as well as see them. So, when a ship comes at you it pushes you back, or it comes in from camera and surprises you.'

Frakes thought it was more interesting to see a section of a ship – an engine or a wing – than the whole thing, while he also wanted Framestore CFC to reflect the energy and excitement that he was trying create on the main shoot. To do this, Framestore CFC tried to include a mix of different camerawork: much of the oil rig sequence looks like it is shot using hand-held cameras, while Thunderbird 2's launch sequence includes a crane shot, and Thunderbird 3 takes off with the 'camera' seemingly attached to the ship itself.

THERE'S NO SMOKE WITHOUT CGI

Creating the huge clouds of smoke generated when Thunderbirds 1, 2 and 3 lift-off from Tracy Island was arguably the greatest challenge faced by Framestore CFC.

Although CGI smoke had been created on other films, with *Thunderbirds* this smoke would have to be bigger and more extensive and the artists at Framestore CFC were not entirely sure how they were going to realise this.

During pre-visualisation, through storyboards and animatics, Framestore CFC had developed a specific understanding of what was required. In discussion with Jonathan Frakes they had developed a sense of how far and how fast the smoke should spread, and how long each launch sequence should run for.

One possibility was to actually recreate these effects through some form of pyrotechnics. It would be hard to capture the look they were going for, however, and combining those shots with the images of the CGI model would be extremely tricky.

Alternatively, they could draw the smoke frame by frame. Again, this would be very hard to do. The slightest mistake would have spoiled the entire effect.

FLUID DYNAMICS

Particle system programs are a key weapon in the armoury of all effects houses. They are used to recreate the way things look in the real world: how a rock would bounce and roll if dropped on the ground, for example, or how clouds of dust swirl in the wind.

Using a Space Shuttle launch as a key reference point, and the way in which its clouds of exhaust move and roll, the CGI effects artists began planning how to recreate this movement with a particle system. It soon became obvious that this kind of movement was too complex to be captured by a standard particle system – they would need to introduce some enhancements.

Engineers have been using programs that model how liquids move for some years. Called fluid dynamics, these programs are able to mimic anything from the currents in the sea to the way a dash of milk swirls and spreads when added to a cup of tea.

By the time the effects team had begun working on the launch sequences, the 3D modellers had finished animating the movement of the vehicles. The effects team studied these sequences and fed them into their own particle system programs. They could feed in where the smoke was being emitted from, what it was going to hit and where the ground was – in effect they were recreating a virtual geography on their computer models.

Alongside this virtual geography, the effects artists also needed to feed in how fast and how many particles should be emitted from each Thunderbird's engines.

PUFFING IT UP

After showing this result to the director and getting his approval, the next step was to turn each of those particles into puffs of smoke. There were, once again, a number of choices available to the team. One approach would have been to take pictures of balls of smoke and place them on each particle. It was felt, however, that the eye would have noticed similarities between different areas of smoke. This was where the need for fractals came in.

Fractal geometry was invented in the 1970s by Benoit B Mandelbrot. Fractals are a mathematical way of describing non-geometric shapes, like those that occur in nature: stones, mountains, clouds or even puffs of smoke.

Using this concept, each dot in Framestore CFC's particle system became the centre of a fractal-generated cloud of smoke. Each dot would have a very dense centre and then get increasingly transparent as it appeared to be further away.

Looking again at shots of the Space Shuttle, the effects team also noticed that each ball of smoke started small, expanded rapidly, and then dissipated. They were keen to recreate this in the launch sequence as well and did so by making the properties of each smoke ball change as time passed.

Gradually, step-by-step, the Thunderbird launch sequences began to take shape. The effects artist replicates the geometry of the Thunderbird 2 launch pad on his computer. This results in a virtual representation of where the ship's engines are, where the ground is, and where the launch ramp and blast shield is.

A particle system, enhanced by fluid dynamics, is run inside this virtual geometry. To get a better idea of the shape of the particle system, each dot is made to form the centre of a sphere.

Using fractals, smoke balls are created, with each puff of smoke centred around a single dot. Each smoke ball is then made to change, grow and then dissipate over a series of frames.

PROFILE JUSTIN MARTIN – FX SUPERVISOR

Whenever you see a shot that includes smoke, dust, water, or the heat haze generated by the engines of the Thunderbird craft, that is a sequence in which Justin Martin's team has been involved.

Jonathan Frakes wanted the film to be eco-friendly and was aware that, with these ships blasting off all the time, by rights Tracy Island should be a burning cinder. As they developed the smoke that was to accompany the launches of Thunderbirds 1, 2 and 3, the team was often asked to make it less dirty. 'We had to make it clean,' says Martin. 'Make it nice, friendly smoke!'

Prior to his supervisory role on *Thunderbirds*, Martin was involved on such productions as *The Matrix* (1999), *Harry Potter and the Chamber of Secrets* (2002), *Blade II* (2002) and *Mission Impossible II* (2002).

Sample
Final Beauty Render

Sample
OcclusionPass

Sample
OcclusionPass

Sample
DerivedDepthMap

PROFILE JONATHAN FAWKNER –
2D SUPERVISOR

Numerous individuals were responsible for
generating the various CG ingredients that went
into the *Thunderbirds* melting pot. However,
it was Jonathan Fawkner's team that was
responsible for taking all these elements
and combining them together so that they
worked as one entity. Since joining
Framestore CFC, Jonathan has worked
on most of the company's major projects,
including the first *Tomb Raider* movie,
two *Harry Potter* films and *Blade II*.

PROFILE FIONA CHILTON –
SENIOR VISUAL EFFECTS PRODUCER

Fiona Chilton gained her first film industry experience
in her native Australia. Fiona worked for the
renowned effects house Animal Logic from
the mid to late-90s, serving as visual effects
producer on *Babe: Pig in the City* and
The Matrix. Other credits include
Mousehunt and *The Thin Red Line*.
She joined Framestore CFC in 1999
and has since been involved with
Chicken Run, *Resident Evil* and *Harry
Potter and the Chamber of Secrets*.

COMPOSITING

The pre-visualisation work and the animatics had given Jonathan Frakes, the production team, and Framestore CFC an idea of what they were all aiming to recreate. Once the pre-vis work was completed, each effects sequence was broken down into its separate elements, with each piece of the jigsaw being given to a different individual or team to build and complete. Once all of these pieces were finished, it was then down to the compositor to start putting them all back together.

The Thunderbird 2 sequence was particularly complicated, taking months of planning and preparation. During the location shoot, a number of plate shots had been filmed in order to capture various views of the island. However, the production team had not been able to find a suitable location to represent the area where Thunderbird 2 was to take off.

For this reason, it was decided that the Thunderbird 2 runway should be captured as a matte painting, drawn directly onto computer by one of Framestore CFC's effects artists.

The next issue surrounded the palm trees that were to fold down on either side of the runway as Thunderbird 2 was transported onto its launch pad. It was agreed that these would be shot on the Pinewood lot during production. They would be filmed in front of a blue screen and lit in the same way as the matte painting and Thunderbird 2. Each of these palm tree sequences then needed to be placed on the matte painting.

Thunderbird 2, sat on top of its transporter, had also been rendered as a separate image. Frame by frame, this too had to be put into place, and positioned in front of, and behind, the various palm trees.

Finally, the smoke effects also had to be generated as a separate element and these too needed to be placed in position. Only then would the whole sequence be of a piece.

DESIGNING THE LAUNCH SEQUENCE

The elements that make up the Thunderbird 2 launch sequence were designed relatively late in the production. When it came to reimagining the launch pad, Framestore CFC wanted the design to reflect the size and weight of the craft it was to lift up. In search of inspiration, they looked at a book called *Big Machines*. The book included pictures of

Sample
Final 2d Rendered Smoke

Sample
Interactive Lighting Pass

Sample
Rendered Dust

Sample
Derived Shadows

PROFILE LUCY KILLICK – VISUAL EFFECTS PRODUCER

Thunderbirds marks Lucy Killick's first credit as visual effects producer. Born in Australia and educated in Europe and America, Lucy was production manager for Financial Times Television before making her first foray into the world of visual effects. Since joining Framestore CFC, Lucy has worked on such diverse productions as *A Christmas Carol*, *The Mummy Returns*, *Dinotopia* and *Harry Potter and the Chamber of Secrets*.

huge bulldozers and tractors, together with a vast machine called a Bucket Loader that is sometimes used in mining. They also referenced NASA's Crawler-Transporter, the huge vehicle that is used to carry the Space Shuttle, and other spacecraft, to NASA's launchpad.

Perhaps the most exciting element of this sequence is the speed with which the launch pad raises Thunderbird 2 into position. The reason for this dynamic movement is actually quite prosaic: Framestore CFC had only been assigned so much of the film's running time for this action to take place. The launch pad had to rise that fast for all the different elements of the sequence to be squeezed into the time allowed.

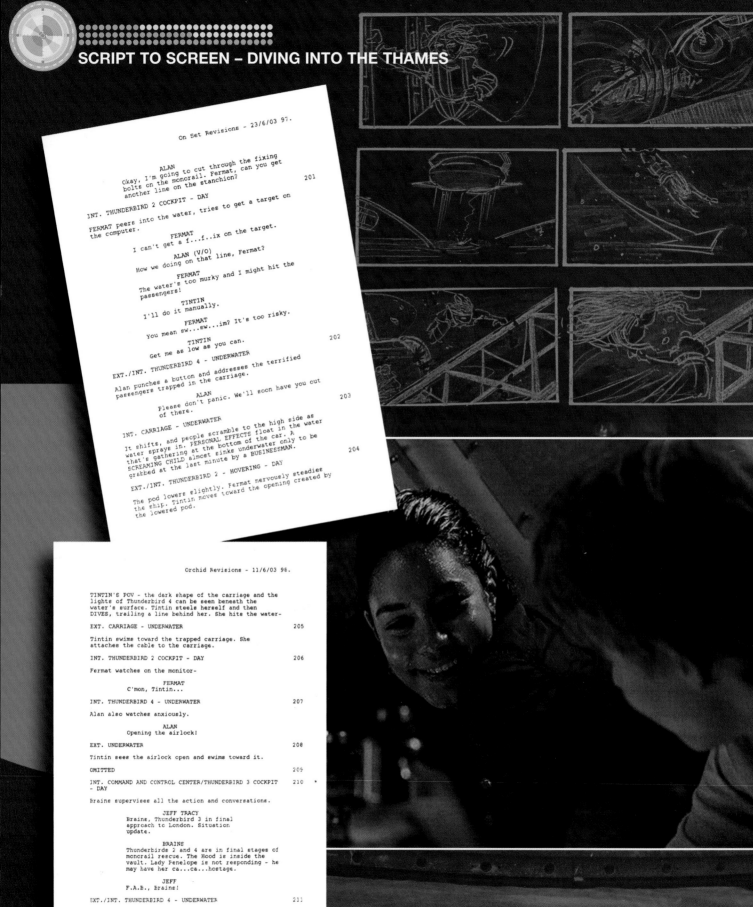

On Set Revisions - 23/6/03 97.

                        ALAN
        Okay, I'm going to cut through the fixing
        bolts on the monorail. Fermat, can you get
        another line on the stanchion?   201

INT. THUNDERBIRD 2 COCKPIT - DAY

FERMAT peers into the water, tries to get a target on
the computer.

                        FERMAT
        I can't get a f...f...ix on the target.

                        ALAN (V/O)
        How we doing on that line, Fermat?

                        FERMAT
        The water's too murky and I might hit the
        passengers!

                        TINTIN
        I'll do it manually.

                        FERMAT
        You mean sw...sw...im? It's too risky.

                        TINTIN
        Get me as low as you can.   202

EXT./INT. THUNDERBIRD 4 - UNDERWATER

Alan punches a button and addresses the terrified
passengers trapped in the carriage.

                        ALAN
        Please don't panic. We'll soon have you out
        of there.   203

INT. CARRIAGE - UNDERWATER

It shifts, and people scramble to the high side as
water sprays in. PERSONAL EFFECTS float in the water
that's gathering at the bottom of the car. A
SCREAMING CHILD almost sinks underwater only to be
grabbed at the last minute by a BUSINESSMAN.   204

EXT./INT. THUNDERBIRD 2 - HOVERING - DAY

The pod lowers slightly. Fermat nervously steadies
the ship. Tintin moves toward the opening created by
the lowered pod.

Orchid Revisions - 11/6/03 98.

TINTIN'S POV - the dark shape of the carriage and the
lights of Thunderbird 4 can be seen beneath the
water's surface. Tintin steels herself and then
DIVES, trailing a line behind her. She hits the water-

EXT. CARRIAGE - UNDERWATER   205

Tintin swims toward the trapped carriage. She
attaches the cable to the carriage.

INT. THUNDERBIRD 2 COCKPIT - DAY   206

Fermat watches on the monitor-

                        FERMAT
                C'mon, Tintin...

INT. THUNDERBIRD 4 - UNDERWATER   207

Alan also watches anxiously.

                        ALAN
                Opening the airlock!

EXT. UNDERWATER   208

Tintin sees the airlock open and swims toward it.

OMITTED   209

INT. COMMAND AND CONTROL CENTER/THUNDERBIRD 3 COCKPIT   210   *
- DAY

Brains supervises all the action and conversations.

                        JEFF TRACY
                Brains, Thunderbird 3 in final
                approach to London. Situation
                update.

                        BRAINS
                Thunderbirds 2 and 4 are in final stages of
                monorail rescue. The Hood is inside the
                vault. Lady Penelope is not responding - he
                may have her ca...ca...hostage.

                        JEFF
                F.A.B., Brains!

EXT./INT. THUNDERBIRD 4 - UNDERWATER   211

Tintin enters and sits beside Alan.

DIVING INTO THE THAMES

Having returned control to Thunderbird 5, Alan Tracy and his friends race to London to prevent The Hood from destroying International Rescue's reputation.

Alan is still inexperienced at flying, but with Fermat's guidance they land at London's Jubilee Gardens with only a slight jolt. 'Textbook, boys,' commends Lady Penelope.

The Hood and his minions are already making their way to the Bank of London. They are using the Mole to travel under the Thames and drill their way into the bank's vault.

Despite Transom's warnings, as the Mole burrows away it passes through one of the stanchions supporting the London Monorail. The result is catastrophic. A monorail carriage is travelling above the Thames just as the stanchion collapses. The carriage falls into the river below and quickly begins to sink.

Flying Thunderbird 2 over the Thames, Alan realises he needs to get closer to the stricken carriage. Leaving Fermat in the pilot's seat he heads down to Thunderbird 4 and launches the submersible into the Thames.

Reviewing the situation underwater, Alan realises that a cable needs to be harnessed to the carriage. Fermat agrees, but can't see what he is firing at. Tin-Tin volunteers to dive into the Thames and manually fastens the cable in place.

It's a long drop, but Tin-Tin's time on Tracy Island has been well spent and she is a very good swimmer. She attaches the cable and swims to Thunderbird 4's airlock.

With Fermat taking the strain from above and Alan lifting the carriage with Thunderbird 4, the desperate passengers are quickly brought to the river's surface. Disaster has been averted – now it is time to stop The Hood…

VANESSA HUDGENS

Being allergic to chlorine, Vanessa Hudgens hadn't learned to swim before she won the role of Tin-Tin. Having read excerpts from the script that included scenes of Tin-Tin in the sea around Tracy Island, Vanessa's parents decided it was time to enrol her in swimming classes. It was just as well: had she not been able to take to the waves Vanessa would not have been given the part.

Vanessa was born in a tiny town in Oregon. Her parents noticed her talent when she was three, and her family accordingly moved firstly to San Diego, and later to Los Angeles. The decision was well made: in 1998 Vanessa had a major role in the stage version of Dr Seuss' *How the Grinch Stole Christmas!* and – long before being cast in *Thunderbirds* – appeared in a dozen commercials and a couple of TV series.

Vanessa's first major break as an actress came when she was cast in *Thirteen*, alongside Brady Corbet. The chance to play Tin-Tin in *Thunderbirds* came soon after.

TIN–TIN BELAGANT

The daughter of Kyrano and Onaha (Jeff Tracy's inestimable housekeepers) and the niece of The Hood, Tin-Tin Belagant had a privileged upbringing. Although her early life was spent in Malaysia, Tin-Tin's family moved to Tracy Island when she was very young.

International Rescue had saved her father's life after a calamitous mining disaster and Jeff Tracy had taken a particular interest in Kyrano's well being. Once his recovery was complete, Jeff invited Kyrano and his family to come and work for him on Tracy Island, and he had offered to pay for Tin-Tin's education.

It was on Tracy Island, however, that Tin-Tin was happiest. Only Gordon Tracy was her equal in the waters surrounding the island, and no one knew the jungle as well as her.

The sea and wildlife were not Tracy Island's only attraction. Tin-Tin recognised that she had feelings for Alan Tracy long before he did, but it was only during The Hood's attack that these became more tangible. During conversations with Lady Penelope, Tin-Tin had been told she would have to be patient with Alan. Finally, her long wait was paying off.

LEX SHRAPNEL

'Lex Shrapnel!' yelled Jonathan Frakes when Lex arrived at his audition for the role of John Tracy. Amused by Shrapnel's name, Frakes simply couldn't help himself.

Of all the Tracy brothers, excluding Brady Corbet, Shrapnel was certainly the most experienced. Prior to *Thunderbirds* he had spent six months filming *K-19: The Widowmaker* with Harrison Ford. Reflecting on his time on the movie, Shrapnel said he knew things were going well when Ford approached him after their first scene together. The scene included a line about eating fruit to stave off radiation poisoning. 'Kid,' said Ford, 'you just managed to turn one of the corniest lines in the movie into one of the best.'

Born into a family of actors, Shrapnel's father, John, was also in *K-19*, while his grandmother is Deborah Kerr. Lex is also a distant descendent of Henry Shrapnel, the eighteenth century inventor of the shrapnel shell.

JOHN TRACY

The oldest of the Tracy brothers, John was 12 years old when his mother died. It was perhaps inevitable that he would became a little quieter and more introspective than his siblings.

His mother's death forced John to grow up quickly: he felt responsible for his other brothers while he also wanted to support his father. As a consequence, the pair became very close and, when on their own, they would often discuss problems or difficulties that they were facing. The tensions between Jeff and Alan were a case in point.

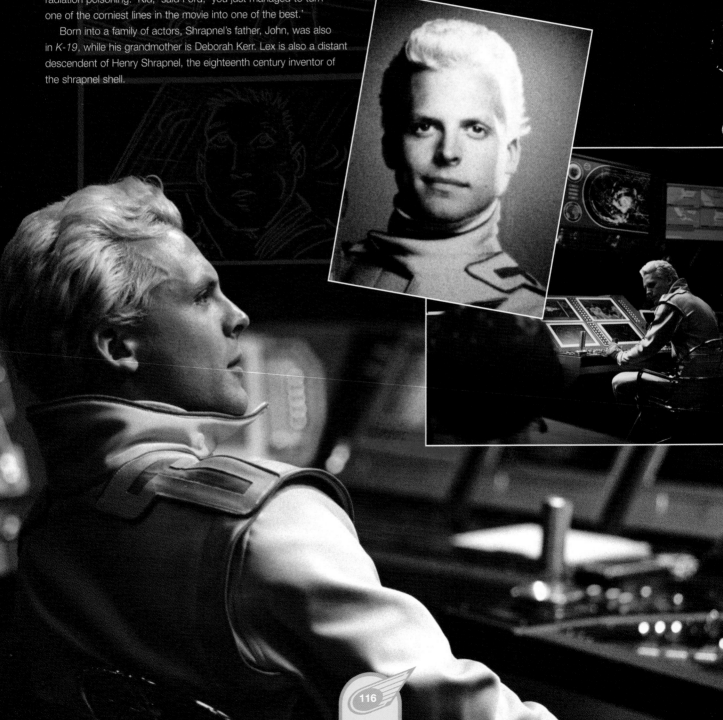

THE THUNDERIZER

Disaster victims are trapped in a tall building with no obvious means of escape. The Thunderbirds are not able to draw close for risk of damaging the building even further. What can they possibly do to help?

International Rescue has just the thing. The Thunderizer boasts some of the most advanced equipment in International Rescue's entire arsenal. Its main feature is a particle cannon capable of firing a web of lasers to disintegrate anything at which it is targeted. Extremely precise, it is possible to program the Thunderizer to cut out holes in walls or even steel doors. When Alan, Tin-Tin and Fermat were escaping from Mullion, Alan used the Thunderizer to cut through the blast doors to the Thunderbird 1 silo.

When buildings collapse, the Thunderizer can be used to cut through the fallen brick and stone, the lasers causing the rock to evaporate. The infra-red cameras on board the vehicle are used to pinpoint survivors and make sure that they aren't hit by the lasers.

OIL RIG RESCUE

The oil rig rescue was one of the most demanding effects sequences in the whole film, and the story of its development is intriguing and complex.

The film's script gave plenty of latitude for how this part of the action should be depicted. Following discussions with Jonathan Frakes, it was left to Craig Lyn and Martin Macrae to flesh out the sequence. They started by simply throwing ideas down onto post-it notes and then shuffling them around to see how the action moved and flowed.

It was at this point that the digital animatics came into their own. Over four or five days, the pair translated their ideas onto a computer, developing a very rough account of the action, what kind of shots and camera angles were going to be needed, and providing a better idea of timing.

Once finished, the sequence was sent to Michael McCullers to write appropriate dialogue. Frakes, his assistant Tanya Phegan, and a couple of the effects artists recorded this and added it onto the soundtrack.

Gradually, the complexity and difficulty of the sequence began to increase. Early on in the film's editing it was decided to ditch the bike race sequence and move the oil rig rescue up to the front of the movie.

At one point the rescue was also going to take place in daylight, but

Frakes suggested instead that there shoud be a stormy night-time setting: 'I wanted it to be dark and I wanted it to be dangerous.'

Interestingly, the oil rig rescue was the only sequence in the movie in which a traditional model miniature was used. No half-measures were taken and a 40-foot scale model of the rig was built for the sequence. Visual effects supervisor Mike McGee explains why they decided not to simply build the rig on the computer: 'There was such a lot of pyrotechnics exploding and oil and flames burning that we knew we had to capture the way light interacted with the rest of the structure. The glows, the backlighting, and all that detail was best captured through a miniature.'

Shooting the rig took a full week. It was Mark Nelmes' job to make sure that all the shots and camera angles matched those depicted in the animatics sequence. In order to give the model scale, Nelmes also shot pictures of huge fireballs at a high film speed – around a hundred frames per second. Once slowed down, these shots helped emphasise the size of the rig.

Completed footage of the model was added to the mix and light from the rig was used to illuminate the Thunderbirds hovering above. Footage of a stormy sea was added in below. Finally, layers of rain were added behind the model, on the model and in front of it. The camera itself was then made to swing, to give the impression that these were images that had been captured from a helicopter.

OIL RIG OR LAUNCH PAD?

Researching ideas for oil rigs of the future, concept artist Dominic Lavery came across images of an actual sea-worthy launch pad. Called Sea-Launch, this facility is currently being used to fire rockets into space.

The lines of this launch pad are extremely clean and clear. John Beard liked the idea that the oil rigs of the future would have moved away from the giant structures that we know today and so Sea-Launch came to be used as the template for Lavery's concept sketches.

BEN TORGERSEN

Of all the main actors in *Thunderbirds*, Ben Torgersen is more than happy to admit that he is the least experienced. Just 17 when the film was shot, his life before that had been somewhat footloose. His family having criss-crossed the Atlantic four times since he was born, Torgersen has lived in such diverse locations as Stavanger in Norway and Dallas, Texas. It was while he was living in Aberdeen that Torgersen used to watch *Thunderbirds* on television.

Torgersen was introduced to acting by his drama instructor, actor Buck Herron, and it was as a result of Herron's encouragement that he signed up with an agent. Arriving for his audition with Jonathan Frakes, Torgersen remembers stopping dead in his tracks. 'You look very familiar,' he said to Frakes. 'Have we met before?' Jovial to the last, Frakes simply replied, 'Maybe – I've done a little TV.'

GORDON TRACY

When The Hood made his dramatic assault on Tracy Island, Gordon Tracy was 18 years old, only four years older than Alan. Being the second youngest causes Gordon to have some sympathy for his little brother. In the fights and arguments between Alan and his father, he recognises himself from just a few years earlier. Of course, this doesn't stop him from joining his brothers in teasing and baiting the angry youth.

Still relatively inexperienced, Gordon usually allows his father and brothers to take the lead in rescue operations and is generally assigned the role of co-pilot on Thunderbirds 2 and 3.

FEEDING BACK

'I was brought up by Rick Berman, the *Star Trek* producer, who's a real diamonds in the detail kind of guy,' says Frakes, defending his perfectionism. As he approached the end of post-production, Frakes was convinced that Framestore CFC must hate him: 'I give lots and lots of notes, and when I see a shot I look at it frame by frame, making sure it works.'

Fortunately, Frakes' instinct when originally choosing Framestore CFC had been spot on. Visual effects supervisors Mark Nelmes and Mike McGee were similarly meticulous and so ideas were repeatedly sent back to the drawing board as they strove to get the sequences just right.

While Frakes' vision for the overall look of the film was coming into focus, there were two elements that were still outstanding: the movie's editing and its soundtrack.

THUNDERBIRD 5 – LESS IS MORE

'I had a problem with how much stuff was in the atmosphere after Thunderbird 5 was hit by the missile,' says Frakes. 'As Framestore CFC added stuff to the shot that they said was motivated by the explosion, it took your eye away from the beauty of the ship itself.' In response, Frakes kept asking the team to reduce the amount of debris by a half and by a third, so that it wasn't so much of a distraction.

The same was true of the interior shots. For the zero gravity scenes the effects artists had worked hard to include floating debris and to have light reflecting off it in just the right way. However, although this looked great, Frakes again felt that took the focus away from the actors and their dilemma. 'Less is more a lot of times,' he remarks, 'or, as Anthony Edwards says, less is actually less!'

THUNDERBIRD 5

Located in geostationary orbit high above the Earth, Thunderbird 5 monitors communications the world over by tapping into satellites and processing news programmes.

A stay at Thunderbird 5 is very different to a visit to the cramped International Space Station, not to mention the old Russian Mir station. In part, Thunderbird 5's relative comfort is a result of the artificial gravity that the station boasts. Using the same anti-gravity technologies that help Thunderbirds 1, 2 and 3 to take off and land, Thunderbird 5's gravity means that visitors can stay on board for indefinite periods and not suffer any major health risks.

Manned by just one of the Tracy brothers at a time, it is John that does the lion's share of the duty. Alternating each month with one of his other brothers – except Alan – John spends six months a year in space. He actually enjoys the opportunity this gives him to spend time on his own.

It is obviously vital for Thunderbird 5's profile to the Earth to be as small as possible. Because of its size, it would not be hard to see the station with the naked eye, and International Rescue is concerned that people should not be able to detect it. The station is accordingly equipped with cloaking systems that conceal it both from radar and other satellites.

SOLAR PANEL ARRAY
While solar panels on most space stations comprise rectangular panels on long arms, Thunderbird 5's panels are located on a circular array resting on the uppermost side of the station. In large part, Brains chose this design because having the array closer to the body of the station limited the amount of light that would be reflected down onto the Earth's surface.

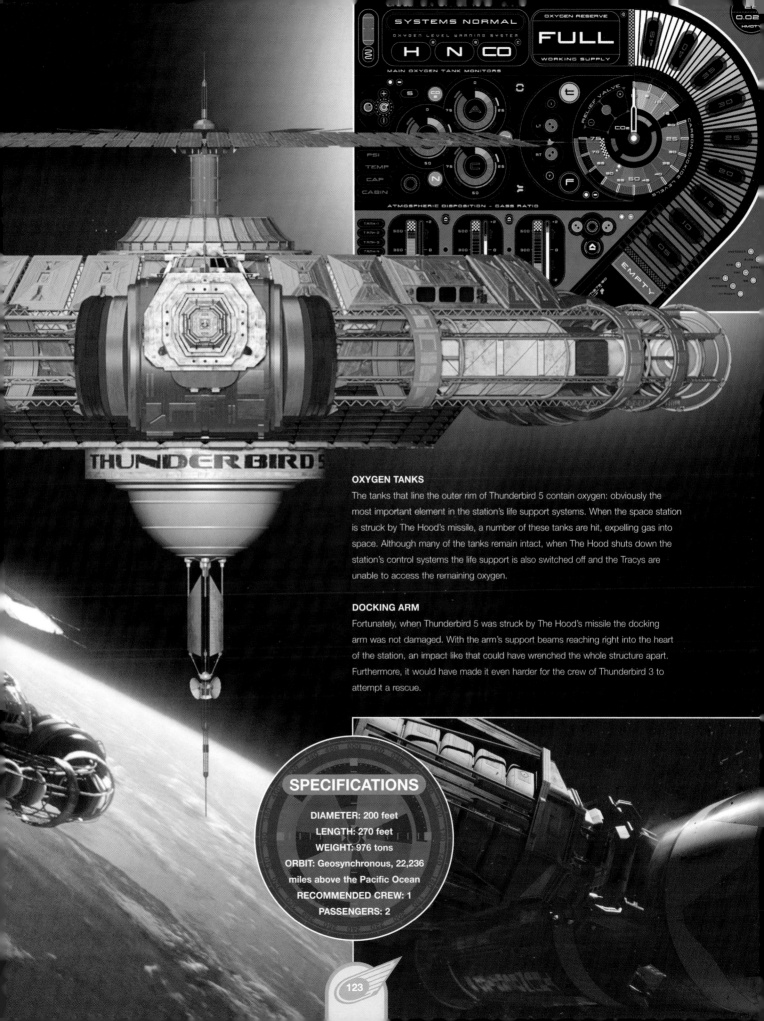

SYSTEMS NORMAL
OXYGEN LEVEL WARNING SYSTEM
H N CO

OXYGEN RESERVE
FULL
WORKING SUPPLY

MAIN OXYGEN TANK MONITORS

PSI
TEMP
CAP
CABIN

RELIEF VALVE
CO₂

CARBON DIOXIDE LEVELS

ATMOSPHERIC DISPOSITION - GASS RATIO

TANK-1
TANK-2
TANK-3
TANK-4

EMPTY

THUNDERBIRD 5

OXYGEN TANKS

The tanks that line the outer rim of Thunderbird 5 contain oxygen: obviously the most important element in the station's life support systems. When the space station is struck by The Hood's missile, a number of these tanks are hit, expelling gas into space. Although many of the tanks remain intact, when The Hood shuts down the station's control systems the life support is also switched off and the Tracys are unable to access the remaining oxygen.

DOCKING ARM

Fortunately, when Thunderbird 5 was struck by The Hood's missile the docking arm was not damaged. With the arm's support beams reaching right into the heart of the station, an impact like that could have wrenched the whole structure apart. Furthermore, it would have made it even harder for the crew of Thunderbird 3 to attempt a rescue.

SPECIFICATIONS

DIAMETER: 200 feet
LENGTH: 270 feet
WEIGHT: 976 tons
ORBIT: Geosynchronous, 22,236 miles above the Pacific Ocean
RECOMMENDED CREW: 1
PASSENGERS: 2

EDITING

Right from the very start, Jonathan Frakes wanted
Thunderbirds to be an energetic, fast-paced movie. 'Kids
have an incredible ability to take in information and not be
distracted by pace. They've learned this from all the time
they spend on video games and watching MTV. They're
tactile – they get bored with long beautiful shots.'

An early casualty on the altar of speed was the bike
race in which Alan competes with his fellow students in
a dash round the school. Upon reflection, it was felt that
this sequence delayed the start of the story proper.
Frakes was keen to ditch it and start introducing
the Thunderbirds right away.

This wasn't the only major sequence to end up
on the fabled cutting room floor. Parker and Lady
Penelope's arrival at Tracy Island after it had been taken
over by The Hood was also lost. In this scene FAB 1 landed
on the sea and turned into a boat. It was then fired upon by
The Hood's submarine and the pair were forced to abandon ship,
arriving on the beach in a pink pedalo.

Although this was a great scene with some fantastic
gags, on reflection it diverted the audience's attention
away from Alan and his predicament.

GAGGING FOR IT

A number of ideas and visual jokes were discussed but never made it to the final edit. One such gag involved Thunderbird 2's final approach to London. As it passed over the Greater London Authority building – occupied by the Mayor of London – the team had talked about having the glass of the building shatter.

Ultimately, they decided to do without this scene. The team recognised that only half the people in London would recognise the building, and only half of *them* would find the joke funny. And, of course, there was also the little matter of cost. This decision didn't mean that the building would be ignored altogether, however. As Thunderbird 2 flies over, its reflection is captured, fleetingly, in the

glass. As Frakes himself says, 'the diamond is in the detail'.

The editing could also be used to skip over things which slowed the movie down. After landing in Jubilee Gardens, how do our three heroes get into and out of Thunderbird 2? What's more, how does the rest of the Tracy family clamber out of Thunderbird 3? Surely they'd need an 80 foot ladder? The fast, dramatic pace distracts the audience from such logical considerations.

Frakes was keen to place Alan at the centre of the film and emphasise his relationship with Tin-Tin. Achieving this was rather like piecing together a vast, multi-dimensional jigsaw puzzle. Gradually, however, a clear picture began to emerge.

PROFILEMARTIN WALSH – EDITOR

Responsible for the editing of such dramas as *Iris* (2001) and *Bridget Jones's Diary* (2002), Martin Walsh might not have been the obvious choice for a movie like *Thunderbirds*. Were it not, that is, for his Oscar™-winning work on the musical *Chicago* (2002).

The relentless pace of *Thunderbirds*, with its rapid cuts and unbridled energy, required a special talent and the success of *Chicago* proved to Frakes that Walsh was the man he needed.

Walsh himself is slightly bemused by his prestigious award. He feels that good editing should be invisible, yet this was certainly not the case with Rob Marshall's film version of the stage musical. 'The only reason I'm suddenly getting all this attention is because the editing in *Chicago* is deliberately part of the show,' he says.

Walsh's role on *Thunderbirds* began with him reviewing all the rushes – each day's footage – and selecting the best material. Once filming was over Walsh then sat down with Frakes, went through this footage, and began splicing the movie together.

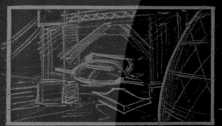
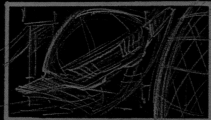
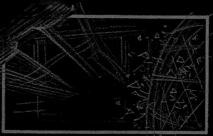

PROFILE HANS ZIMMER – COMPOSER

Nominated for seven Oscars™ and the winner of one, for *The Lion King* (1994), German-born Hans Zimmer is one of the most well respected composers in the modern day film industry.

A prolific writer of film scores, Zimmer has been responsible for the music of *Gladiator* (2000), *Thin Red Line* (1998) and *Rain Man* (1988). A pioneer in the use of synthesisers, advanced computer technology and electronic keyboards, Zimmer is expert at combining these elements with the sound of a traditional orchestra. In the early days of his career, Zimmer was involved in the writing of the synth-pop hit 'Video Killed the Radio Star' and also produced an album for the group Buggles.

As well as continuing to work as a film composer, Zimmer has more recently become the head of DreamWorks' music department, making him the first composer to hold such a position in a major studio for several decades.

CREATING THE SOUND OF MUSIC

As the movie took shape, Frakes began preparing for the first test screenings. It is common practice in the film industry to prepare a temporary soundtrack for such screenings by borrowing appropriate sounds and music from other films and splicing them into place.

Generally, this wasn't difficult to do. When directing the *Star Trek* films, which always use the music of Jerry Goldsmith, it was easy to lift appropriate music from previous films in the series. Once again, however, Frakes was having to come to terms with the very strange beast that *Thunderbirds* was shaping up to be.

'Because we change tone so often and so rapidly,' says Frakes, 'and because it feels a little like *Spy Kids*, it feels a little bit like a Bond movie, or the original Supermarionation series, it was very difficult to find music that sounds appropriate throughout.'

As a consequence, the temporary soundtrack they came up with was very much a patchwork. In some places a bit of *Spiderman* worked, in others they tried *Galaxy Quest* or even bits of *Indiana Jones* for the straight ahead hero sequences.

Frakes had asked the Oscar™-winning composer Hans Zimmer to write the soundtrack to the film. He had to wait until the middle of January 2004, just six months before the film's release, to get his first taste of what Zimmer was going to come up with.

Listening to this for the first time, Frakes and his companions breathed a collective sigh of relief. With the film so varied and so fast it needed an original score to lend it some more cohesion.

THE GAMBLE PAYS OFF

Working Title and Jonathan Frakes had decided to breath new life into one of the most beloved British television series ever made. They had a huge amount to live up to. Fans of the series had huge expectations of any revival, while everyone that had grown up with the series would also want their memories of it to be honoured.

As they revived a project previously put aside in 1997, Working Title took some significant risks. They invited Jonathan Frakes – a newcomer to the British film industry – to take the helm and he built a whole new team from scratch.

Working alongside Universal and Working Title, Framestore CFC created more effects than any British facility had ever handled. In addition, Framestore CFC were asked to work in partnership with the design team and to undertake pre-visualisation work.

Thunderbirds was a unique television series, and the same can be said of the movie. With a heady mixture of space, underwater and aerial effects sequences, together with an incredibly fast pace, making all the elements work together was always going to be difficult.

With Hans Zimmer's musical score finished and the last CGI elements complete, the film was finally ready. Fans had waited almost 40 years for *Thunderbirds* to return and the film itself had taken two years to produce. At last the wait was over – finally, the time had come for *Thunderbirds* to face its audience.

ABOUT THE AUTHOR

Film and television journalist Andrew Darling has written for various genre titles including *SFX* and the official *Star Trek*, *Star Wars* and *Babylon 5* magazines. He is also a regular contributor to the *Official Star Wars Fact File* partwork series. *Thunderbirds: The Making of the Movie* is his first book.

ABOUT THE DESIGNER

Since graduating in 1996, James King has worked as a graphic designer on numerous book and magazine projects. He was part of the team that created the *Official Star Wars Fact File*, and has since designed books on such diverse subjects as Pink Floyd, Halle Berry and The Marx Brothers.

PICTURE CREDITS

Our special thanks to Cindy Chang and Kate Wyhowska for their help in providing the vast majority of the stills used in this book. Our thanks also to Framestore CFC for supplying images that appear on pages 10-11, 18, 25, 32, 37, 89, 108-109 and 110-111, and to Rex Features for images that appear on pages 62, 63 and 126.